A SILICON VALLEY LIFE

What I learned from the birth of the transistor to the age of Apple and Amazon

Edited by Pattie Sellers,
SellersEaston Media, January, 2022

to Jean
and my three sons

TABLE OF CONTENTS

Foreword

by Mark, Damon, and Todd Kvamme

Part of growing up as the three sons of E. Floyd Kvamme was comprehending, gradually over time, what great impact our father had.

In the 1960s, he worked alongside the wildly innovative pioneers of the semiconductor industry. Starting in 1963 as a product marketing manager at Fairchild Semiconductor, he moved quickly into sales, where his engineering expertise and principled, matter-of-fact approach to problem-solving made him a standout performer. By the '70s, when we were growing up, he was at National Semiconductor, ushering in the emergence of mass market semiconductors while creating some of the first consumer electronics launching the new digital age.

In the early 1980s, our dad was present at the creation of the Macintosh. He worked with Steve Jobs, Apple's founder and creative genius, and grew close to him, acting as a personal advisor on all sorts of things. In 1984, when Apple introduced the computer that would transform the way we work and live and learn, our father played a key role in the Mac launch strategy.

And in the mid-'80s when our dad moved to Kleiner Perkins Caufield & Byers, the venture capital firm that funded startups like Google and Amazon, he seemed to possess a sixth sense about where the tech industry was heading. He was constantly eager to learn from the world's smartest, most creative people and pass on the lessons he learned. He did exactly that for George W. Bush when, in 2001, he signed on as one of the President's top technology advisors.

Now we realize that our father has had an extraordinary career. But when we were just three kids of a hardworking tech executive in a place not yet famous as "Silicon Valley," Floyd Kvamme was, to us, just "Dad."

And what an amazing dad he was! While he frequently traveled the world for work (tirelessly wooing customers in Europe and Japan), he managed to be totally present for us. Home for dinner at 7 o'clock— always greeting us with his jubilant "Hi hi!" and giving our mom a kiss. We began dinner by thanking God for our food, and then he would ask, "What did you guys do today?" Tennis and baseball—and our annual ski vacations—were the topics of dinner talk. Dad let us have the stage, and he listened intently.

He always helped us with our homework—even in college! We relied on him to help us get our heads around assignments to design logic circuits and build electronic brains. He was patient and brilliant, and we came to understand how his engineering prowess and passion drove his business success.

That passion for engineering—his insatiable desire to understand and communicate how things work—is the essence of this book.

Long before our mom passed away in September 2020, she would frequently prod our dad with "You should write a book." We had no idea he was working on it until one day when he pulled out a couple of chapters. "Dad, this is good stuff!" Mark told him. Dad took it from there and wrote a book that we believe is valuable reading for any business leader today.

This book is jam-packed with concise, practical lessons on how to sell (Chapter 3: The Elevator Pitch), how to prioritize your workload (Chapter 7: Balance: Rocks in a Jar), how to build successful businesses in the most competitive global markets (Chapter 11: Five Fingers), and how to handle bad news (Chapter 19: If You're Going to Take a Bath, Get Clean), and how to build loyal high-performing teams (Chapter 24: Speaking the Truth in Love… at Work).

This book brings to light the difference between knowledge and wisdom. Knowledge is facts and figures and data, which we need more than ever in this data-driven world. But facts and data are easy to get—thanks to the industries that our dad played a key role in building. Wisdom is the application and interpretation of knowledge. Great wisdom is a rare and much more valuable thing. Our dad's book is loaded with great wisdom.

The three of us have followed in our dad's footsteps. Todd and Damon, like dad, earned degrees in engineering and have continued on that path in the Valley. And like Dad, Mark worked in marketing at Apple and then made his way to venture capital. Mark has invited Dad to speak to groups of CEOs in his investment portfolio, and every time these people have found his stories—essentially stories of leadership—both relatable and helpful to their own business-building.

As Dad's sons, we've benefited from his wisdom for decades, and we believe it deserves much wider exposure.

Introduction

I WAS BORN ON DECEMBER 8, 1937, at Mary's Help Hospital on Guerrero Street in San Francisco. I didn't have to travel far to get to my first home. It was a small rental apartment across the street from the hospital. My parents, Magnus and Erikka Kvamme, lived there with my brother Harold, who was 17 months older than me. My father had immigrated to America from Norway 12 years before, in 1925 when he was 19 years old. My mother, who also grew up in Norway, came to the United States in 1930 when she was 17. My mother and father met in church and quickly fell in love. They married in 1935 and started their American family.

Since they had arrived in the U.S. as young adults, my parents had no educational experiences here. They had come to join other family members who had arrived before them—to places in Wisconsin and Washington state, as well as California. To put food on the table and support their young families, my Norwegian relatives worked in the trades that they knew back home. This included carpentry, which was my father's trade.

He was a small but muscular man, as strong as an ox, and a proud member of the Carpenters Union—Local 22 in San Francisco. Until my mother became his bride, she made her living as a domestic worker, cleaning homes and doing basic kitchen duties. Both my parents worked hard and without complaint, even though neither made a lot of money. Their social life was simple and centered on the church. They attended both Glad Tidings Church on Webster Street and Bethel Temple (now Bethel Christian Church) on Capp Street in the Mission District.

That small rental apartment on Guerrero Street was our home until I turned two years old, and we moved to an actual house in San Francisco's Sunset District. Our new home was a row house at 1743 29th Avenue. The house had been built by the company that my father was working for. Even though it was narrow in the front—each lot was just 25 feet in width—our new home was much more spacious than the apartment. The lots were 110 feet in length, and that gave Harold and me room to spread out and play.

It was a diverse neighborhood with lots of friendly neighbors. Most of the families were Italian, but we also had neighbors who were Irish, African American, and other ethnicities. Because the row houses were connected—with adjoining walls separating each home from the homes on each side—you could hear the neighbors' music and baseball games that played on their radios. On quiet nights, when we were supposed to be in bed and fast asleep, Harold and I would listen through our bedroom wall to the San Francisco Seals baseball games.

Many of the children in our neighborhood attended Catholic school. Harold and I went to public school, starting with kindergarten through sixth grade at Lawton School. It was an easy two-block walk from our home to our school on Lawton Street, and Harold and I walked back and forth together every day. Some people thought Harold and I were twins—particularly after he fell ill and got behind in his classes, and the principal moved him back a grade. Harold didn't mind being in my grade, and I felt the same. He and I were best friends, and as we saw it, the more time we could spend together, the better.

Sunset Playground was our favorite place in the neighborhood. It was down the street from our house, between 29th and 28th Avenues and Moraga and Lawton Streets. The playground took up a full city block, with swings and slides and fields for baseball, football, and other sports. After school let out and our homework was done, Harold and I would spend our remaining available hours at Sunset Playground. The superintendent, Barnie Greenberg, loved sports, could play any and every sport, and taught us how to play baseball and football. If not for Barnie Greenberg, I might never have learned these sports because our dad knew nothing about American sports.

Sunset Playground kept Harold and me and many other children occupied with good, wholesome recreation. Barnie, the superintendent, wanted everyone, regardless of athletic ability, to play and have fun. So in touch football matches and baseball games, he often joined the younger children on their team and helped them compete with the older boys. Harold and I were always on Barnie's team, and we frequently won. Oftentimes, these games ended when we heard our mother call out our front window: "Harold and Floyd!" That meant it was dinnertime.

Our family quickly grew to five children. My sister Ruth was born three years after me. Then came Gordon, two years after Ruth in 1942. The Kvamme family's post-World War II baby, Ardis, was born in 1946. Even though Harold and I were best friends, I got along with all my siblings. As I moved into my teen years, I came to be known as the studious one. My favorite book was The World Almanac and Book of Facts. Every year, a new issue came out, listing details about world events and sports feats. Each year, I saved up my money to buy the new edition.

I was a serious and diligent high school student, interested in playing sports but able to fit just two into my schedule. Near the end of my junior year at Jefferson Union High in Daly City, the football coach asked me to come out for spring training. He had been my gym instructor. He knew my athletic abilities, and he thought I would make a good backup quarterback. I was both flattered and wary, knowing that the primary quarterback was far better than I was. But I agreed to give it a try. I worked out with the team several times after school until I realized that the packed regimen of practices and games was not going to sync with my other responsibility: a newspaper delivery business that was my means of making money to pay for college.

Just as I was about to tell the coach that I needed to quit, the decision was made for me. One afternoon as we were practicing "Hail Mary" pass plays, I was throwing the ball. I was supposed to keep the ball in my hands until the last possible second, to give my ends adequate time to get past the defensive line. As I faded back to pass the ball, two defensive ends—beefy, bulked up seniors on the varsity squad—charged and hit me. I went down hard with the ball. Those two muscle-bound seniors were Jack Thur and John Madden. Yes, the John Madden. The famous football coach and sportscaster graduated a year ahead of me at Jefferson Union High. He later became the school's legendary alum.

My other high school sport was track and field. At the start of my senior year, Mr. Ribera, my math teacher who was also the track coach, asked me to join the track team. He wanted me to run the half mile and the full mile. Our school was in a very competitive league, and I hardly distinguished myself or contributed to our record. But I enjoyed the spirit of camaraderie. This was 1955, and during one race, a fellow named Don Bowden, a star runner who went to another school in our area, broke the U.S. high school record for the half mile. Two years later, Don became the first American to run a mile in less than four minutes. Out of my experience running and watching amazing athletes like Don, I developed an interest in track and field that endures to this day. While I enjoy the strategy of baseball, I get a real thrill from watching the amazing speed of runners on the track.

My First Job

WITH LIMITED TIME for sports, I focused on my priorities, which included helping out with our family finances. Starting at 14, I helped my mother do our annual tax returns. Managing receipts and preparing the paperwork for the Internal Revenue Service was her job, and she appreciated my giving her a hand. I never considered the work any sort of a sacrifice. I loved math and the challenge of getting my head around all those big numbers. They were actually not big numbers. My father never made enough to set aside money to pay for my siblings and me to go to college. If I was going to do that—and I certainly planned to—I would be paying my own tuition.

Our family culture centered on hard work, self-sufficiency, and generosity. Our family's work ethic was grounded in my parents' upbringings: My father grew up on a farm in Norway, where he and his 12 siblings were assigned chores that they had to perform daily. My mother was one of 13 children as well. Her father was a Norwegian boat builder, and most of her brothers were fishermen. When the boats came in with a full catch, there was plenty to do to prepare the fish for market. My mother and her sisters got their hands dirty. They could clean a fish in no time.

My parents passed that work ethic and spirit of generosity on to all their children. Their habitual generosity tended to challenge our family's financial stability, however. My folks were so generous that anyone who came to our front door got a handout—food or money or something else that would help them out. My mother was always good for a $20 handout—which was a very hefty sum in the 1940s. During World War II, when our relatives back in Norway were suffering under Germany's invasion and the Nazi occupation, my mother sent countless care packages to her relatives and friends.

It was, in fact, my industrious mother who got me into the newspaper delivery business. In 1946, she learned that the San Francisco Call-Bulletin, our city's biggest afternoon newspaper, was looking for newsboys to make deliveries Monday through Friday. My mother inquired and was told that two routes were available. This was great for Harold, who was 10 years old, but I was only nine—one year too young to qualify for a route. My mother devised a clever workaround: She took two newspaper routes under Harold's name, and she gave me one of them.

My route covered six blocks on 24th avenue from Judah Street to Pacheco Street in San Francisco's Sunset District. Five days a week, the delivery man would drop stacks of Call-Bulletin newspapers at a service station at 24th and Judah Street. I'd walk straight from school to pick them up, untie them, load them in my newsboy carrier bag, and set out to deliver them to the doorsteps of about 60 local customers.

Delivering the papers was the easy part of the job. The real challenge— and the valuable business learning—came from working hard to collect payments from customers at the end of each month. Here's how it worked: I paid money up front to purchase the Call-Bulletin newspapers. So, I owned them. At the end of each month, I collected $1.25 from each of my customers. If a customer didn't pay me, it was my loss.

My incentive to collect was extremely high. That $1.25 per month price was a set rate regardless of whether customers got 20 newspapers in a month, as they did in February, or 23 newspapers, as they did in the seven months of the year that contain 31 days. I paid the Call-Bulletin four cents per newspaper, as I recall, so my monthly income per customer was between 33 cents and 45 cents, with an average 40 cents per customer per month. Delivering 60 papers meant that I earned $24 in a month. That doesn't sound like much, but remember, this was the

1940s. My carpenter father earned only about $100 a week. The $24 that I brought in monthly was serious income.

My income went primarily into the piggy bank for my college education. I learned early on the basics of money management—plus lessons in other areas such as marketing and customer service. For instance, Harold and I agreed that we would always deliver the papers right at the front door so the customer didn't have to walk outside to retrieve the paper. We got great tips for our exceptional service. Ten cents seemed fantastic when we were netting 40 cents a month per customer. At Christmastime, we got dollar tips from some of our customers. Those tips sure added up.

Our burgeoning business had to adapt in 1949, when I was 11 years old, and we moved again. This time further away—to the Westlake District of Daly City, just miles south of San Francisco. My parents bought the house because this new development was being built by the company my father worked for, the Henry Doelger Company. Doelger, a San Francisco-based builder, had bought some 600 acres of sand dunes and cabbage patches between Daly City's western edge and the Pacific Ocean. The Henry Doelger Company created a community called Westlake. It was annexed to Daly City in 1948.

Since Westlake was quite a ways out of the city, Henry Doelger provided incentives for his employees to become owners. My parents jumped at the opportunity, pulling together their meager finances to buy. Meanwhile, I learned that the Call-Bulletin, as well as the other San Francisco newspapers, were seeking to build a robust clientele of subscribers in this fast-growing new residential community. The morning papers, the San Francisco Examiner and San Francisco Chronicle, were long established and bigger than the Call-Bulletin, the afternoon paper, so I figured that delivering either of them could be a lucrative endeavor. I would have to get up very early each morning, but that's a small price to pay to build a major business.

I got up at 3:45 in the morning five days a week. Monday through Friday, as soon as I finished delivering my papers around six o'clock, I would rush home, crawl back into bed, and sleep for one more hour before I had to get up for school. On Sunday mornings, my mother helped Harold and me handle the extra-fat editions, bulging with ads from popular stores like Sears and J.C. Penney. My mother would drive around Westlake in her Pontiac, delivering some of our papers for us.

I discovered that building a successful business requires not only hard work, but also careful strategy and robust innovation. When I realized that many of the people who were moving into Westlake were not from

the San Francisco Bay area—and therefore not current subscribers to the San Francisco newspapers—I talked with the man in charge of hiring the newsboys. I explained to him that my father, a foreman for the Henry Doelger Company, had access to data on new homeowners— who they were, where they bought, and when they were scheduled to move into their new homes. I suggested an idea to him: If the San Francisco Examiner would give me one full month of free newspapers for each new Westlake homeowner, Harold and I would deliver the papers to them, starting on their move-in day, for no charge. Then, at the end of the month, Harold and I would call on each new homeowner and ask them if they would like to continue to receive the newspaper, delivered every day right to their front door.

Left: In the 1960s and '70s, this Transistor Manual, containing several chapters that I wrote, became the bible of transistor design. Publications about transistors and electronic products boomed during this era.

The man in charge of the newsboys agreed to let us try out our idea. It worked like a charm. Nearly 50% of Westlake's first 700 homeowners signed up for delivery—which was wildly impressive given that just 10 to 15% of homeowners in San Francisco had signed up for delivery. Examiner subscribers paid $2 per month for seven-day-a-week delivery. Harold's and my income from each customer turned out to be about 60 cents per month. The first section of homes in Westlake earned us about $180 per month. As Westlake built more homes rapidly, we offered the free 30-day trial to every new resident—and when our business got too big for us to handle by ourselves, the Examiner created new routes. We got to the point where we were delivering about 300 papers each morning.

Our business really did help to support our family. And we found that what our parents told us about generosity—"if you give, you get in return"—was true. When my mother was short on cash, she would often borrow from us. She paid us back at interest rates of her choosing, often in the teens. Sometimes we didn't even realize that she was taking cash out of our pouch until we would find she had deposited a few extra dollars for us.

I'm forever thankful for the business education that I got as a boy. I gained a good understanding of how businesses get built, how the economy works, and how to make a profit.

Political Involvement

I LEARNED ABOUT POLITICS from my parents who, as soon as they arrived in America as teenagers, longed to be productive and proud U.S. citizens. They learned English quickly—and always spoke English, not Norwegian, in our home. They gave my four siblings and me American-sounding names. My actual name is Earl Floyd Kvamme, but after giving me that name at birth, my parents decided they didn't like Earl. They apparently called me "baby" until I was about two years old—when one day my father came home from work and called me "Floyd." He liked the name because Floyd Gibbon, then a popular man on radio, was his favorite newscaster. The name Floyd stuck.

To stay up to date on politics and the national issues of the day, my parents read the San Francisco News, another afternoon paper, and listened to Floyd Gibbon and other radio commentators. My father was a solid Union Democrat, as were his carpenter friends in the Local 22. In 1948, when I was 10 years old, my father was for Harry Truman in the presidential race. All the newspapers were predicting that Thomas Dewey, the Republican nominee, was going to win. On Election Night, as we crowded around our Scottie radio to listen to reports on the early returns, I got excited because Truman was reportedly doing well. I walked into my parents' bedroom to tell my dad about the surprising news. He assured me that my enthusiasm was misplaced and that the returns were too early to predict anything.

Harry Truman won that 1948 presidential race. The next morning, the front page of the Chicago Daily Tribune proclaimed "Dewey Defeats Truman" in a banner headline that was terribly premature and notoriously incorrect.

Seeing such political drama on the national scale got me interested in participating at another level of politics; at my elementary school. At Lawton, there were essentially two student bodies, kindergarten through third grade, and grades four to six. Each student body had a government meant to cultivate the students' interest in public affairs. Each student body elected the officers, including a president whose job, among others, was to make announcements at assembly meetings. In the third grade, I became a candidate for president of the K-3 student body. My friends and I created campaign materials and a presentation on my qualifications to lead the K-3 student body—all very serious stuff! My campaign theme: "Vote for Kvamme or I'll tell your mommy." This message won the election for me.

That early experience—campaigning and serving as president of my kindergarten-to-third grade student body—taught me how to organize a message and talk to groups of people. Even at eight years old, I felt comfortable speaking to a crowd, and that comfort would serve me well in the decades to come.

Faith

I WAS GENERALLY an obedient child, and I rarely challenged the authority of my parents or my teachers. But no kid is an angel, of course. I remember one time when I was about seven years old, my brother Harold and I were in a five & dime store on Noriega Street, near our house. We were wandering around the store when I saw a small toy that I wanted to buy. I didn't have the money to pay for it, so I picked it up and put it in my pocket. My mom learned of my theft after we got home, and she saw the toy. She then marched me back to the store to apologize. She didn't get angry. Instead, she calmly explained to me that what I had done was wrong. She walked me back to the store and had me confess to the lady at the checkout counter what I had done. I had to tell the lady that I was sorry and promise her that I would never steal again. The whole experience was humiliating, but it worked. I never stole another thing.

Faith was an anchor then, as it has been ever since. We rarely missed Sunday School and Sunday church—typically attending Sunday morning and evening. Tuesday night was adult Bible Study, which our parents attended most weeks. Once we were old enough, my brother and sisters and I went to Youth Night every Friday. Run by young members of the congregation, Youth Night was designed for people ages 13 to 35. Really, it offered something for everyone—particularly people in their late teens.

I found all the church activities valuable in terms of shaping my code of conduct. Christian belief came naturally to me, and while I had questions (Where do the stars come from? How did the moon come to be?), the Christian answers seemed logical to me. As I studied science in high school and then college, the order I saw in the universe seemed to require a grand designer. That reinforced my beliefs. And the compassion

I saw in many situations in nature drew me to see God as a Personal Being who had created everything and set it in motion.

As I grew into adulthood, some of my friends wondered how I lived with the prohibitions of Christianity—all the things you "should not do" that seemed to them inhibiting and constricting. I never looked at Christian doctrine that way. If my parents recommended that I not do something, it seemed logical to me to seriously consider their point of view. As a result, I didn't attend a movie until I was 21 years old. (One of my early and all-time favorite movies: A Man for All Seasons.). I have never smoked a cigarette in my life. To coin an old phase of the time when I was growing up, I didn't "smoke, drink, or chew, or go with girls that do." On Friday nights, after the youth service, my church friends and I would go out in groups of eight or 10, often to Fisherman's Wharf to get ice cream or Cokes. One-on-one dating was something of a rarity. I dated a bit, but exclusively girls in the church because they were the ones I felt most comfortable being with.

I found some degree of career direction one day when my high school English teacher, Mr. Thomas Redmond, asked me about my plans for the future. I told him that I might want to become a teacher. He didn't throw that idea out, but he asked me if I had considered engineering. I said I really didn't know anything about it. Engineering, he explained, is applied mathematics—and he knew that I loved mathematics. After that, I started looking into engineering schools. I had no idea what type of engineering I should consider, but I decided that the University of California at Berkeley was my first choice.

I applied to Berkeley, and I got in. I majored in electrical engineering because, I was told, it involves mathematics more than any other type of engineering. Those four years at Berkeley, I focused on my studies much more than any sort of social life or the dating scene, and my college experience was fine but pretty uneventful, except for playing football for our House team, where we won a couple of championships in intramural play between residence halls.

I lived at a University Co-op called Cloyne Court on the north side of campus. Almost all the students living in the co-op were there for one reason: It was cheap. In exchange for room and board, residents committed to work five hours a week at the house, and for a low fee, they received all their meals and lodging. The managers of the co-op were very much on the left politically. We would have incredible debates about virtually all the political issues of the day. This atmosphere helped me develop the center-right positions I hold to this day on most issues.

At Cloyne Court, I also got a good feel for the arguments used by the left to sell their positions. Several of my housemates were in on the founding of SLATE, the first campus political party. Some played a role in establishing the Student Nonviolent Coordinating Committee (SNCC) at Berkeley, and participated in the foment on the Berkeley campus later in the 1960s. In that house, I also learned to listen and take in opposing viewpoints. The political atmosphere was so charged that at the beginning of my senior year, my housemates on both sides of the political aisle elected me House Judge to handle disputes.

Just before graduation, something changed my life. Our church youth group went on a ski trip to Dodge Ridge Ski Area in the Sierra Nevada mountains. I was there with a date who was a platonic friend. I learned that a girl in another youth group was having difficulty picking up skiing, and as it turned out, I knew her from back home. I'm certainly no expert on the slopes, but I took the opportunity to show this girl some essential aspects of skiing and give her some advice. She was beautiful and bubbly and funny—a girl who, I could tell, tended to look at the bright possibilities in every challenge and could always get things done. She and I hit it off big-time.

The girl was Melba Jean Thompson, and like me, she went by her middle name, Jean. Our relationship developed quickly, and neither she nor I wanted people to know about our affection for one another. So we kept our relationship a secret. Within a few months, I was thinking that this girl could be my wife. One Sunday at church, Jean and I announced our engagement, and the congregation was stunned. Virtually no one saw it coming. They didn't even know that we were dating.

On June 20, 1959, 10 days after I graduated from Berkeley, Jean and I wed. Our marriage endured for more than 60 years, grounded in a shared faith that has served us well through the good, the bad, and the ugly. I lost Jean to a horrible form of cancer in 2020.

Choice of Profession

NEWLY ARMED WITH A B.S. in Electrical Engineering from Berkeley, I moved with Jean to Ventura, California, for a job at Electronic Systems Development Company, a small supplier of systems to the aerospace industry. The company was founded by two German scientists and did most of its projects in support of work at Point Mugu Naval Air Station nearby. It took only a few months at the company, where I was designing electronic systems with transistors, for me to realize that it would be smart for me to pursue a Master's degree in this exciting new field of semiconductors. I applied to the Master's in Science program at Syracuse University, which was one of the only such programs in the U.S. (I chose Syracuse after writing to some 30 universities and learning that only Syracuse and Purdue had MS programs with a semiconductor focus.) I was accepted. So, Jean and I packed up, drove our 1953 Oldsmobile across the country, and rented a flat in Syracuse.

The Master's program, sponsored by General Electric's Syracuse-based

GENERAL ⊛ ELECTRIC

COMPANY

ELECTRONICS PARK, SYRACUSE, NEW YORK . . . TELEPHONE GRanite 6-4411

ELECTRONIC COMPONENTS

DIVISION

SEMICONDUCTOR PRODUCTS
DEPARTMENT

Electronics Park
July 25, 1960

AIR MAIL SPECIAL DELIVERY

Mr. E. F. Kvamme
310 South Brent
Ventura, California

Dear Floyd:

As a result of your interviews with us last week, we would like to extend an invitation to you to join us as an Engineer in our Semiconductor Rotating Assignment Program at a starting salary rate of $8,100.00 per year, paid weekly. Your first assignment would be with Evaluation Engineering, Mr. R. P. Frenzel, Manager.

We will also reimburse you for your relocation expenses from Ventura, California, to Syracuse, New York. These expenses include packing, moving, and unpacking of your household goods and living and travel expenses for you and your wife. The Internal Revenue Service considers such monetary compensation as personal income which is subject to Federal income taxation. We would suggest that you and your wife come to Syracuse a few days prior to the date you report for work for the purpose of locating suitable housing; any expenses you may incur during that time in connection with house hunting would also be reimbursed.

At the time you report for work, it will be necessary for you to successfully complete a physical examination given by our local Company physician as well as present your birth certificate and Social Security card.

We are certain you will find the work opportunities here in the Semiconductor Products Department to be highly creative, challenging, and rewarding; and we are looking forward to a favorable response to our invitation.

If you have any questions, please do not hesitate to call me collect at GRanite 6-4411, Ext. 3100.

Very truly yours,

W. E. Wendt/bw

W. E. Wendt, Specialist
Manpower Development
SEMICONDUCTOR PRODUCTS DEPT.

WEW:bw

*In 1960, General Electric hired me as an engineer in its
Semiconductor program. My salary was $8,100.*

28

CIRCUIT
DESIGN
ENGINEERING

MACTIER PUBLISHING CORPORATION • 17 East 54th Street, New York 22, N. Y. • PLaza 2-7620

November 20, 1962

Mr. E. Floyd Kvamme
Semiconductor Products Dept.
General Electric Company
Syracuse, New York

Dear Mr. Kvamme:

Enclosed is our check in the amount of $62.50, representing
your honorarium for the article by you and Mr. Davidsohn
which appeared in our September issue.

Thank you for making this article available to us for
publication.

Sincerely,

Elmer T. Ebersol
Elmer T. Ebersol
Editor

ETE:ec

Enclosure - Check #3017
          Amount $62.50

Two years later, I got paid $62.50 for an article that I wrote.
As Jean and I started to build our family, every cent helped!

Semiconductor Products Division, offered mostly night classes. During the day, I worked in the applications engineering department of GE's Semiconductor Division, designing with transistors, and in the evening, I went to my classes and studied as much as I could. Jean was pregnant at this point, and in February 1961, she delivered our first child, Mark.

This was a wonderful time for us, with a new baby and so much learning about new technologies that would likely change the world. At GE, I worked on the GE Transistor Manual, which explained how semiconductors work. In fact, I wrote a significant portion of the 1960 edition, which became somewhat of a bible in the semiconductor business. Semiconductors were new, and I had developed enough of an expertise to lecture across the country about how to use this potentially transformational innovation.

I found my job at GE fulfilling. The problem was that the company had all sorts of rules about promotions; GE systematically planned your career for you. I found the rules too restrictive, particularly at a time when technology was advancing so quickly and shifting the demand for jobs and fields of expertise. Who knew, in this dynamic marketplace, what the best jobs of tomorrow might be?

Jean was always flexible and willing to move anywhere. So in 1962, armed with my Master's Degree from Syracuse, Jean and one-year-old Mark and I moved back to California. I spent a year working as an electronic systems design engineer at Space Technology Labs in Redondo Beach. The so-called space race, a competition between the United States and the Soviet Union to explore outer space, fascinated me. The legendary "race" had begun on October 4, 1957, when the Soviets launched Sputnik, the world's first artificial satellite. By 1962, it was an intense technology-driven rivalry. I was excited to help America win this race—until Space Technology Labs lost its contract over a legal matter. The company transferred me to a ground-based project, which wasn't nearly as interesting.

I knew something else out there would excite me more. And in April 1963, I found it. I joined Fairchild Semiconductor as a Product Marketing Manager. Founded in 1957 as a division of Fairchild Camera and Instrument, Fairchild Semiconductor was a pioneer in the manufacturing of transistors and created the first silicon integrated circuit. My boss assigned me to work with companies looking to buy semiconductor products for their computers or other electronic systems. This was an exciting new adventure as Jean and two-year-old Mark and I moved to Mountain View, close to Fairchild's headquarters. So began my journey in what came to be called Silicon Valley.

The balance of this book contains a number of stories and lots of ideas that I picked up while working in the Valley. There are stories that I hope will make you laugh. There are stories about certain ideas that were helpful to me as I advanced in my career from two companies that were present at the creation of Silicon Valley, Fairchild Semiconductor and National Semiconductor, to an exciting startup called Apple Computer, to a prodigious venture capital firm, Kleiner Perkins Caufield & Byers, that played a major role in creating the Silicon Valley that we know today.

These stories involve real people I had the pleasure of working with during my 60 years of Valley experience. My memory is not perfect… by a long shot. The wonders of the web enabled me to research the facts and figures behind the stories I tell, but as we all know, neither Wikipedia nor the mass media gets it right all the time. I apologize in advance for any incorrect details, and I take responsibility for the errors. For those of you who were there in Silicon Valley, particularly in the early days, I hope this book brings back pleasant memories. It's been a great run and a very fun ride.

National Semiconductor Corporation

DM7890 DM8590/DM5400 7400N decade counter

general description

Monolithic decade counter capable of counting
pulses at a guaranteed frequency of 20 MHz.
Gating is also provided to asynchronously reset
the counter to the BCD Counts of zero and nine.

Open Operation

DM7890 DM8590 SN5404 SN7414
BCD to decimal decoder drive drive

absolute maximum ratings

- Supply Voltage V_{CC}
- Output Voltage
- Input Voltage
- Operating Temperature Range DM7890 0°C to +75°C
  DM8590 -55°C to +125°C
- Storage Temperature Range -65°C to +150°C

- TTL 74 Series
  Gates
  Flip Flop
  MSI
- DTL 930 Series
  Gates
  Flip
- MOS
  Register

Information

EMC / NS

The Beginning

National Semiconductor's display at our first conference in Tokyo in 1967

CHAPTER 1

The Valley Circa 1963

I STARTED AT FAIRCHILD Semiconductor as a product marketing manager overseeing Custom Integrated Circuit projects. My job was to obtain orders from clients who didn't want our standard products, but instead wanted us to design custom products for their specific needs. Many of these clients were computer companies that were beginning to see the value of using silicon-based integrated electronics in their systems. My work included monitoring progress through weekly or biweekly review sessions, which took place at Fairchild's Research and Development Laboratory in Palo Alto.

The Fairchild R&D Lab was a fascinating place. So was the man who managed the facility, Gordon Moore. Today, Gordon Moore is renowned as a Silicon Valley entrepreneur who co-founded two Fortune 500 companies, Fairchild Semiconductor and Intel, and came up with Moore's Law, which holds that computer processing power doubles every two years. In fact, it was on April 19, 1965, while Gordon was Director of the R&D lab that Electronics magazine published an article by Gordon called "Cramming More Components onto Integrated Circuits." In the article, Gordon noted that the number of transistors that could be placed inexpensively on an integrated circuit doubled approximately every two years. He predicted that this trend would continue. A few years later, the press named Gordon's observation "Moore's Law."

I got to know Gordon when he was not yet legendary, but I knew from the start that he was brilliant. He was so smart in perceiving what was going on in the nascent computer industry, and what that would lead to in terms of market trends and demand for semiconductors. Gordon had studied chemistry at the University of California, Berkeley, and then earned a Ph.D. in chemistry and physics from the California Institute of Technology (Caltech) in Pasadena. That background equipped him to understand, differently from the way most engineers understood, the physical composition of semiconductors and the ways they were becoming more powerful. As innovation was happening at a fast and furious pace, Gordon was an ideal lab director. He had a quick mind, and whatever the challenge or obstacle, he seemed to be unflappable.

We all had a sense that we were at the start of a revolution. We believed that the semiconductors we were designing and producing could change the ways people work and live their daily lives. Semiconductors, we knew, would make everything from toasters to TVs, from cars to washing machines, run better and faster. Moreover, given that this activity was happening six years after Sputnik had signaled that the U.S. was behind in the space race, our new technology offered America great new hope.

Many members of the Fairchild Semiconductor R&D team were foreign national immigrants. I've always believed that the reason for this was that back then in the 1960s, most electronic design in the United States was being done for defense purposes. Engineers who were not U.S. citizens typically were not allowed to work on these projects. So they chose to work in commercial companies that were not wholly dedicated to defense work. I don't have exact figures, but I would guess that approximately 40 to 50 percent of the R&D technical staff personnel were foreign-born. In fact, two members of the founding team of Fairchild Semiconductor, Jean Hoerni and Eugene Kleiner, were born outside the U.S.

Fairchild Semiconductor was founded in 1957 by these two immigrants, Gordon Moore, and five other technical people. They had all worked for the inventor of the transistor, William Shockley, at Shockley Semiconductor Laboratory in Mountain View. Reportedly, Shockley lost their services when his authoritarian management style created such friction that their best move was to leave and start their own company. The eight men ended up taking an offer from an east coast military/aerospace contractor, Fairchild Camera and Instrument Corporation. Via this transaction, their startup was called Fairchild Semiconductor, and it was a wholly owned subsidiary of Fairchild Camera and Instrument, headquartered in Syosset, Long Island, New York. The history books call the entrepreneurial group of disaffected PhDs "the traitorous eight."

Their scheme worked, and Fairchild Semiconductor quickly became the leader in the fast-growing semiconductor industry. From their start, the founders decided to work exclusively with silicon. This was a smart decision. While transistors were traditionally made using germanium as the starting material, silicon was essential to making complex integrated circuits and meeting the temperature range required in most aerospace systems. Germanium transistors were generally guaranteed to operate in ambient temperature environments up to 71 degrees Celsius. Silicon could be used in temperatures as high as 125 degrees Celsius.

Fairchild Semiconductor used silicon technology to design the first monolithic integrated circuit, and the company's patented Planar Technology was the foundation of more advanced integrated circuits used in government missile and space agency projects. These space projects, which I worked on when I was promoted to Sales Engineer in

1964, included the Apollo Guidance Computer. This was the computer installed in each Apollo Command Module and Apollo Lunar Module. It was powered by a dual-three input NOR gate containing only six transistors—a far cry from today's chips that can contain millions, if not billions, of transistors.

As I moved into the Sales Engineer role, I got greater exposure to the broad base of talent across Fairchild Semiconductor. It was extraordinary. Fairchild's engineers were the talk of the industry and dominated most conferences where semiconductor technology was on the table for discussion. Our General Manager was one of the company's founders, Dr. Robert Noyce, who was known as Bob. He was an affable man of deep technical capability. At the R&D lab in Palo Alto, Gordon Moore's staff was the "who's who" of silicon technology. His team included Dr. Robert (Bob) Seeds, Dr. Andy Grove, Tom Klein, Roger Smullen, and scores of other technical pioneers who later made giant contributions to advance the tech industry.

Beyond the lab, Fairchild's operations were also known for having exceptionally strong talent. Charlie Sporck was in charge of manufacturing. Fred Bialek ran the autonomous diode plant in San Rafael, California. Tom Bay headed marketing and sales, while Don Valentine led the sales force. Fairchild's Regional Managers were W. J. (Jerry) Sanders in the West; Bernie Marren in the Midwest, Jim Martin on the East coast, and Marshall Cox in the Southwest. At Fairchild's chip design operation inside our Mountain View plant, Bob Widlar was producing world-class analog integrated circuits. (You'll read more about Bob in Chapter 31.). Bob Graham ran product marketing, where I started. (I remember sitting in Gordon Moore's office one morning in November 1963 when Bob Graham stuck his head in the door to tell us that President Kennedy had been shot in Dallas.)

To motivate its employees, Fairchild issued generous stock options.

313 FAIRCHILD DRIVE, MOUNTAIN VIEW, CALIFORNIA 94041 · (415) 962-5011 · TWX: 910-379-6435 · CABLE ADDRESS: FAIRSEMCO

October 14, 1966

Mrs. Floyd Kvamme
810 Rubia Drive
Sunnyvale, California

Dear Jeannie:

During the recent Sales Conference in Acapulco, I
made a clutch of candid photographs for our "souvenir"
brochure. Of the entire collection, I feel the best
I made was the shot of Floyd.

I thought you might like to have a copy of it.

Cordially,

Ricardo J. Alfaro II
Marketing Services

RJA:ca

enc.

My lifelong global travel started in 1966 with travel to Fairchild Semiconductor's Sales Conference in Acapulco.

Top: Sharing expertise at a tech conference.
Bottom: National Semiconductor won a contract to supply ACDelco with
semiconductors for automobiles.

National Semiconductor executives and directors. National thrived under CEO Charlie Sporck, who had quit Fairchild in a mass executive exodus that included Bob Noyce and Gordon Moore (co-founders of Intel) and Advanced Micro Devices founder Jerry Sanders.

The idea was that every employee was going to be an owner. Inside the company, it felt that way. Fairchild took the salesforce to annual conferences in fancy places like Hawaii, Acapulco, Mexico, and Puerto Rico. The salespeople felt like winners, and we all felt like we were members of the best team in the burgeoning semiconductor industry.

A few years later, a new technology, MOS (Metal Oxide Silicon) transistors, began to attract attention. Using MOS instead of bipolar transistors in an integrated circuit's basic switching unit held the promise of fitting many more transistors on a single chip. Fairchild wasn't ready for this technology transition. While the company had led the industry as an "all silicon" house, it was falling behind competitors in this transition from bipolar devices to MOS devices. Moreover, several new companies entered the market, using this new technology to take business away from Fairchild.

While the luster of the Fairchild brand was being tested, flagging financial performance in other divisions of Fairchild Camera and Instrument, the parent company, stirred employee unrest. The stock was not performing well, and rumors of a spinoff of Fairchild Semiconductor persisted. If management in New York didn't know that the troops were restless, they must not have been reading their mail.

The grand exodus began in 1967, and it included extraordinary tech talent. Charlie Sporck left to become CEO of National Semiconductor, a struggling company that he transformed into one of the largest chip makers. The following year, Bob Noyce and Gordon Moore quit Fairchild to start a company that they called Intel. A group led by Jerry Sanders founded Advanced Micro Devices (AMD) in 1969. And once we entered the 1970s, virtually none of the industry-leading technical and marketing talent were still at Fairchild. As they scattered, they created "Silicon Valley" and built the foundation of the tech industry we know today.

What is the lesson in Fairchild's fall? Winners don't stay on sinking ships. Fairchild went from being "the place to be" in the early 1960s to becoming an also-ran company by 1970. The reason for Fairchild's failure was obvious: Top management was not paying proper attention to the stellar talent the company had or to trends that were revolutionizing the industry—and the world.

CHAPTER 2

The Good Thing About Trouble

IN 1964, TWO YEARS AFTER I joined Fairchild Semiconductor as a product marketing engineer, my new job as Sales Engineer took me to Bedford, Massachusetts, outside Boston. At Fairchild's office there, my accounts included the MIT Instrumentation Laboratory (later renamed Draper Labs) and several Raytheon facilities.

This was all very exciting. MIT was designing the moon-bound Apollo computer, among other important navigational computers for space and missile defense systems. In the 1960s, everyone wanted to be part of the Apollo program.

Raytheon's factory in Waltham, Massachusetts, was doing much of the manufacturing, based on the MIT designs. Raytheon had a problem that was quickly becoming my problem: Fairchild's shipments of transistors for an important missile system—the Polaris, as I recall—were not arriving on time. Since I was Fairchild's Sales Engineer on the Raytheon account,

I was called into a meeting in the General Manager's office at Raytheon headquarters in Lexington, Massachusetts. My assignment was to explain our poor delivery performance. Having been in the job for only five weeks, I had not met most of the people in the room. But I quickly realized that these men were the leaders of the facility, and they were not happy with Fairchild. By extension, they weren't happy with me.

The General Manager did most of the talking, and he made clear, in no uncertain terms, that Fairchild Semiconductor had created a major problem in their manufacturing activities. In fact, as I recall the conversation, he even suggested that I, as the overseer of this bad performance, was responsible for harming the defense of the United States. That evening, I told my wife, Jean, that after only five weeks in my new position as sales engineer, I had managed to have a negative impact on national defense!

All laughing aside, we had a problem, and I had to fix it. I worked diligently with our Fairchild team back in California to improve our delivery of the transistors. Fairly quickly, we turned the situation around, and Raytheon was satisfied.

That meeting made a lasting impression on me. There, in the General Manager's office, I learned that when you're in trouble, you get the opportunity to meet very important people. Almost all companies that are in supplier relationships get into trouble at one time or another. The important thing is how you respond to the trouble and recover from it. Think of trouble as your opportunity to step up and lead. Customers will not forget the efforts that you made. Regardless of whether you played a role in creating the problem, a difficult time is an ideal time to make a positive impression.

CHAPTER 3

The Elevator Pitch

THAT MEETING IN THE General Manager's office at Raytheon turned out to be my introduction to the most important people at the Waltham facility. After resolving the delivery problem, I had no contact with the General Manager for the next several months. This changed when I returned to Raytheon to try to secure a major order for integrated circuits for the Apollo computer. After checking in at the Raytheon reception desk, I walked to an elevator bank to go to the third floor, where I had an appointment to meet with the buying group.

As I stepped into the elevator, who did I see but… the General Manager! In our brief two-floor elevator ride, he and I exchanged pleasantries about the weather. As I stepped off the elevator, I uttered a simple "Goodbye."

As I said that, I realized what an opportunity I had just missed. Here I had the General Manager "caged" for an entire two-floor elevator ride, just as I was on my way to close a million-dollar order that he would need to approve! How could I have been so thoughtless—so stupid—to have discussed the weather, never mentioning my reason for my visit to his building? What a mistake I made!

We ended up winning the new contract, which was a very important victory because it was for the Apollo computer. In a pre-win memo to our team, I teed up the rigor of Raytheon's demands of us by writing, "Remember, on Apollo, the customer really is asking for the moon." While I was proud of our success in securing that contract, it took me a long time to stop beating myself up about my lost opportunity on the elevator ride with the GM.

Soon after, Fairchild called me back to California to take a marketing

manager position. I later moved into marketing roles at National Semiconductor and Apple Computer that presented opportunities to speak at sales conferences. At these conferences, I talked about my experience in the Raytheon elevator—and the importance of having an "Elevator Pitch" handy for an unexpected opportunity to explain your product or your service to a potential buyer. At the time, I had never heard anyone else use the expression "Elevator Pitch."

In subsequent years, other people started to use the term "Elevator Pitch," and this phrase was mentioned in several books. Whether these people heard the expression from other sources, I don't know. In any case, the importance of having an elevator pitch cannot be overestimated. In today's world of countless messages and noise and competition for attention, explaining your offering succinctly is more critical than ever.

This point was driven home for me years later when I was working in the White House Office of Science and Technology. For an Energy Report that the President's Council of Advisors on Science and Technology was preparing for President George W. Bush, I was researching websites to learn about new areas of activity in the alternative energy field. Many websites presented homepages that failed to describe the fundamental thing that the company offered. There was lofty language about mission and vision and market opportunity, but no elevator pitch presenting the most vital information. This is a mistake and a lost opportunity.

While I never again had the good fortune of riding an elevator or bumping into that Raytheon General Manager, I learned the value of being prepared for the mission at hand. I believe that an elevator pitch—a concise, compelling, truthful explanation of what you have to offer—should be repeated everywhere a new client may seek information about what you do. Find the essence, communicate it, and valuable relationships can blossom.

CHAPTER 4

Be Bold – Particularly If You Are Young

SELLING CALLS FOR BOLD and creative persuasion. Add a bit of humor, and you might make a sale.

Shortly after I arrived at National Semiconductor, we competed for a large order for integrated circuits to be used in a prototype system to display stock trades in real time. In those days, investment company offices displayed electronic ticker tapes providing up-to-the-moment trades. Our circuits were being used to power a next-generation electronic board.

Winning this order would make National Semiconductor a major supplier of display electronics—a huge boost for our fledgling company. The specification was not easy; it involved integrating high-voltage output drivers to a logic circuit. Early integrated circuits did not like high voltages. To the best of my memory, the customer, GTE's Pennsylvania-based Ultronix division, gave us an order for 150,000 pieces of a "to be designed" driver circuit. This was a very nice addition to our backlog.

The development turned out to be more difficult than we had anticipated, so we were running behind schedule. But we were getting close to success, and a few of the circuits we produced met the specification. Simultaneously with this progress, our sales representative learned that GTE was intending to release another order for an additional 150,000 pieces. We didn't want any of our competitors to move in on our opportunity, so I decided to go out and visit the customer and convince him to give National the new order and double our backlog for the device.

I was about 30 years old at the time. The buyer, Al Glendon, as I recall, was a good deal older. I had never met him until my visit. Our meeting started a bit coolly in that Al was very concerned about our failure to fully deliver his first order on time. And he was skeptical about the ability of our relatively new firm to meet his ongoing needs.

I knew it was time for the bold move. With some flourish, I whipped out two completed units and presented them to him as proof that we were, in fact, capable of building the product he wanted.

Remember, my main objective was to get him to commit the next 150,000 pieces to us as well. While brandishing the two pieces, I mentioned that a major problem was that GTE "hadn't made a big enough commitment to us!" Al leaned back in his chair, laughing at full volume. After he composed himself but still chuckling, he exclaimed, "Floyd, you have the biggest set of clangers I've ever seen. Here, you show up with two pieces against a 150,000-piece order and say that I haven't made a big enough commitment!"

A strange thing happened. Al and I bonded. He appreciated our aggressive pursuit of his business. After several days of additional discussion, Al awarded National Semiconductor the new order. Boldness created a personal relationship and a lucrative order.

A few years later, we were competing for a major order from Interdata, a computer company based in New Jersey. Here, we were the clear underdogs. Our competitor, Texas Instruments, was the incumbent. National Semiconductor had recently introduced a version of the desired circuit, and we thought it had superior performance, but TI was considerably larger than we were and had performed reasonably well in meeting Interdata's requirements. The Interdata representative made a number of trips to California to visit us and scope out our capabilities. He urged us to compete against TI for the new piece of business.

I was asked to come to a meeting at Interdata to help close the deal.

We met with Interdata's engineering and component specialists and then convened in the Purchasing Manager's office. I believe his name was Tom. Well, Tom wasted no time in giving us an answer: "Sorry, you guys have done a great job in bringing your capability to our attention, but we are going to stay with Texas Instruments on this order at this time."

The room fell silent. Our sales representative broke the silence by asking to use the phone. He dialed a number and said, "Phoebe? Hold for a moment, would you?"

Then he turned to the purchasing manager and said, "Tom, you know how hard I've worked on this order. I've traveled back and forth to the coast a number of times at great expense. I've had to be away from my family on many nights. Would you explain to my wife why I lost the order?" He handed the phone to Tom.

A BOLD move. I wouldn't necessarily suggest this tactic to salesmen in most situations, but here, it helped build a relationship that paid off in the long term. No, we did not get that order, but we won a customer for the future. And I bet Tom never forgot that day.

Of course, boldness can go too far. I once witnessed an arrogant applications engineer in a customer meeting with General Electric in Oklahoma City, shouting in frustration, "I know why you are not getting this. You are too dumb to get this!" and then exiting the room. We had to write countless letters of apology—and believe it or not, we got the business since we were in an almost sole source position with GE. But I would never endorse such an application of boldness and stupidity in talking to a potential customer.

Balancing boldness and tact is tricky. Delivering a touch of humor is usually a nice way to tone down the aggression, build a personal relationship, and leave a good lasting impression. This works particularly well if you're young and hungry. I've found that older folks generally want to help new entrants into their industry. In the case of Al Glendon,

I think he wanted me to be successful. He applauded and rewarded my aggressiveness. If you're bold enough to make your meetings memorable—but not offensive—you are making progress.

CHAPTER 5

Advertise What Sells

I NEVER TOOK AN academic course in advertising. So, when it became part of my job to use advertising to attract customers, I had a lot to learn. The go-to-market industry structure in the 1960s included sales engineers, describing in basic terms the features of new semiconductor products, and articles in technical magazines, which detailed how to build computer systems.

Using these new semiconductors in applications such as consumer products (TVs, radios, tape players) and aerospace/defense systems (missile guidance and space exploration) and other industries was a whole new world. Few engineers had college training in semiconductor circuit design. A variety of new circuit design magazines popped up to meet the widespread public curiosity about semiconductors, educate people to use the innovative technology, and prepare people to go into this exciting new field.

Fairchild was in an enviable position. Our company had excellent relationships with distributors, who were the key to making semiconductor products available for designers to try out new designs. Many distributors were headed by young entrepreneurial managers who were not necessarily experts in new technology, but they were good at getting our products to customers.

Schweber Electronics was one of the early standouts. Founded by Seymour Schweber, an outspoken entrepreneur, Schweber Electronics enjoyed a prime position, particularly in its New York home region. On the West Coast, two distributors, Tony Hamilton and Sid Spiegel, had similar lead positions. But it is Seymour I'd like to talk about.

Seymour Schweber "owned" page 3 of Electronic News, a weekly trade newspaper that covered all aspects of the electronics industry, including semiconductors, computers, communications, space, and consumer products like TVs. Everybody read Electronic News. Well, by that I mean everybody in our industry and everybody who wanted to learn about the latest and greatest technology. Seymour's ads were always on the first open page after the cover. And in his ads, an article always accompanied the pictures of the products he was promoting.

Those Schweber Electronics ads used to drive me crazy because Seymour rarely featured the new stuff we were introducing to the market. He focused on assuring his customers that he could meet their needs for standard products that had been on the market for some time. No doubt, that approach helped Seymour build the loyalty of his own customers, but it was not an effective way to increase the sales of our new products. On one of my trips to the East Coast, as I was making plans to meet with Seymour at his Long Island, New York, headquarters, I decided to talk to him about my frustration. My goal was to be polite but candid and straighten him out on his advertising.

Well, I was the one who got straightened out. As soon as I arrived at Seymour's office, he introduced me to the members of his "board." In one corner of his office, Seymour had three or four mannequins seated at a round table. I didn't say a word to Seymour about these oddball characters. Seymour was a fun guy who loved to put on a show, and I figured I would go with his flow.

Seymour told me that his purpose in advertising was not to sell something that is not selling well, but rather to advertise what is selling. He noted that if a product isn't selling, the advertising usually is not to blame. Rather, that poor-performing product is probably missing the market in some way. This was a problem that the greatest advertising in the world can't solve.

"Advertise what's selling," Seymour said. Meaning: Promote the products or services that get clients in the door. Then you can introduce them to all the new widgets and gizmos and fantastic new products that your suppliers have to offer.

Seymour Schweber was right. I've never forgotten his advice. Building a business relationship around what customers know and want is essential, even as you use advertising to pitch products that customers don't yet know. To grow, every business must build both loyalty and excitement. The art of marketing is in the balance.

CHAPTER 6

Automotive Roadblock

EVER SINCE THE DAWN of the semiconductor industry, suppliers have looked to the automotive industry for opportunity. The first successful application of semiconductors in cars was in passenger entertainment systems. Radios have been in cars since 1922. In the 1960s, Ford introduced four- and eight-track cassette players.

Their mediocre sound quality earned the devices mixed reviews. But the growing market for automotive applications led semiconductor companies to pursue more than just entertainment. Semiconductor suppliers dreamed of transforming the guts of the vehicle.

I was at Fairchild Semiconductor in the '60s when I had my first opportunity to sell to the automotive market. A decade earlier, Ford had introduced the Thunderbird to compete against more pricey European cars. The 1955 Thunderbird had power seats and other advanced technology. In 1965, Ford added sequential turn signals, which flashed in sequences from inside to outside across the Thunderbird's horizontal tail lights to indicate a turn. Ford's tech innovations impressed us at Fairchild, and we purchased a rear bumper and associated parts from a Ford dealer and used silicon to design a more sophisticated sequential turn signal mechanism. I pitched our technology to Ford, which passed on adopting what they called a "costly" upgrade to their existing system.

I later visited Ford's Chief Engineer to learn what it might take to break out of being a parts supplier for automotive entertainment systems only. The conversation was friendly and open—and one I will never forget. I asked the engineering chief what applications would be potential areas for semiconductor suppliers. He commented mainly about semiconductor reliability and then opened his desk drawer and took out some sort of mangled automotive part. It was a badly bent piece of metal with gear teeth. Some of the teeth were missing.

He asked me to carefully examine the part and then asked a strange question: "Is this a good part or a bad part?"

The answer was obvious. This mangled piece of metal with missing gear teeth was obviously not functional. "It's a bad part," I told him.

He reached into his drawer again and pulled out a standard semiconductor package: a 16-pin dual inline device. He asked the same question: "Is this a good part or a bad part?"

Of course, I didn't know the answer. I needed a piece of electronic test equipment to know whether this part was functional or not. As I recall, the Chief Engineer went on to explain that in the automotive sector, more than 90% of the "test" was done with the human eye or the human ear. Car owners may not know the function of a failing part, but they can see or hear that it is not working properly.

I was stunned that a company as large as Ford relied on sight and sound to test reliability and performance features. This unsophisticated method of testing left little room for semiconductor suppliers to demonstrate the value of their innovative devices.

The following day, I asked Fairchild's sales representative covering the Chicago area to set me up with Sun Electric, a leader in testing the "electric" parts of automobiles. Sun Electric's executives informed me that essentially no conversations had taken place with the major car manufacturers about investing in advanced electronics. In fact, they were so impressed with my minimal knowledge of the auto industry that they asked me to join the Sun Electric board of directors.

For me, this was a wakeup call that the American auto industry was ignorant about advanced technology opportunities and likely to lose against tech-savvy international competitors. These folks at Ford, as well as other U.S. car companies, should have been investing early in the latest semiconductors. The car companies finally woke up, but it was way too late.

One catalyst for change came a decade later, in 1975. Congress passed CAFE (Corporate Average Fuel Economy) standards, which required manufacturers of automobiles and light trucks to meet certain fuel economy standards. This set in motion urgent meetings between automakers and semiconductor companies. At the Society of Automotive Engineers' first Convergence Conference in Troy, Michigan, the CEO of General Motors spoke about the implications of the new legislation. I presented a paper about semiconductor performance in automotive environments.

This was a turning point in both the automotive and semiconductor industries. By 1980, the Closed Loop Carburetor Control circuit, an electronic control system for carburetors, was standard in various car models. Today, a shortage of semiconductor chips, driven by supply chain problems that started during the global COVID-19 pandemic, is paralyzing automakers. No doubt, as cars become self-driving and ever more energy-efficient machines, they will be in the control of smart semiconductors.

CHAPTER 7

Balance: Rocks in a Jar

PRIORITIZING THE WORKLOAD is a constant problem for managers as well as most professionals. With never-ending pressure to "get things done," prioritization is mandatory. But how do you best do it? Particularly when coming out of the COVID crisis that changed so many of your usual planning norms.

At Fairchild in the 1960s, I remember one application engineer who had two in-baskets on his desk. He labeled one "intense" and the other "not so intense." Most of his incoming mail landed in the "intense" in-basket. That's no surprise. It's a natural habit to try and prioritize everything including the value of a workmate's time. Which means you're prioritizing nothing. And the work keeps loading up.

Solutions to this problem are hard to come by. Locking yourself away in a corner office to focus on a "main" assignment typically doesn't work because direct reports and colleagues need at least some small amount of your attention. Let's say you are the VP of Sales in your company. Your job includes making sure that the product sales group meets its goal. You also need to ensure that the right people call on the right clients—and that your salesforce is up to date on the endless flow of new products coming from the engineering and marketing departments. Plus interruptions about sales plans, proposals to key accounts, and proposed marketing campaigns, not to mention the time related to your son's soccer match, your wife's birthday... The list goes on and on.

How do you prioritize and get it all done while leading a "balanced" life?

You don't get it all done at once. I've found it helpful to apply the popular time management idea of the rock, pebbles, and sand. Let me explain.

First, visualize each area of your life as a rock, a pebble, or a grain of sand. The rocks represent the important things, such as family, faith, and friendships. The pebbles represent your work, your social commitments, and most of your relationships. The grains of sand represent small or minor activities, like taking in a movie or walking the dog or, professionally, thinking about the message you've been considering for next year's product introduction.

Now, think of putting those rocks and pebbles and grains of sand in a jar. Here's the reality: If you start by putting the sand and the small rocks in the jar, the jar will likely get so close to full that the largest rocks won't fit.

Meaning: If you don't focus on your larger priority items first, you may never find time to get to them. You'll be so focused on and driven by peripheral tasks—the pebbles and the sand—that you'll fill up your life with tasks that won't carry you toward your higher goal of living "a balanced life." In fact, if you focus on too many small tasks, you might end up burning the midnight oil to frantically catch up—only to learn that your colleagues moved on without you.

The ideal approach is to put the rocks in the jar first. This assures that, come hell or high water, you will spend priority time on activities that matter today (and maybe every day). Use your spare time, the sand, to check in with your staff, review smaller projects, and just take a break. That break time often triggers your brain to relax and think creatively. Who knows what fresh ideas will emerge?

To get going, spend time assessing what you have done in the recent past and how much time you allotted to it. Include everything—business and pleasure. Are there things that you could just stop doing? If you're replicating what someone else does or if you're doing something not really needed anymore, STOP doing it. If it's a report, stop sending it out. If no one notices, let it be. Move on to more meaningful tasks.

Imagine how much more productive you'll be if you cut in half the time you allocate to your less important tasks. Eventually, you'll come up with a list of your activities of varying importance with a "size" assigned to each. You will focus only on things that matter. And you will enjoy the feeling of fulfillment and balance.

My three sons have taught me about balance. My oldest son, Mark, is a successful venture capitalist who finds time to indulge his passion for auto racing. My middle son, Damon, is a physicist working in the semiconductor capital equipment field who finds time to play several musical instruments and read books constantly. Damon is fluent in French and speaks some Arabic as well. My youngest, Todd, is a mechanical engineer and an authority on all things Disney. He is an avid comic book collector. And he made his daughter's senior prom dress, as well as dresses for his wife and friends. Somehow, as I strived for balance in my life, the effort was contagious, and my three sons have plenty of variety and the satisfaction of balance in their very full lives. I am proud of them for that and more.

Traveling in the cheap seats, National style.
Business travel was pretty much an all-male activity back then.

CHAPTER 8

Breakfast Meetings

SILICON VALLEY BEGAN as a supplier of components—silicon transistors, silicon integrated circuits, and other parts—to the military/ aerospace, computer, industrial, and consumer markets. Unlike today, most of the systems companies were not headquartered in the valley south of San Francisco—the area we know today as Silicon Valley. Many customers traveled across the U.S. from New York State's Long Island, New Jersey, the Boston area, Florida, and Maryland.

By the 1960s, there were about a dozen semiconductor suppliers vying to meet the needs of visiting systems companies. Fairchild Semiconductor was "king of the Valley" and usually got preferential treatment from visitors. For Fairchild and every other supplier courting customers and potential new customers, the most-wanted calendar slot was dinner on an out-of-town visitor's last day. A dinner meeting on a prospective buyer's final day was, of course, the ideal opportunity to close a deal. The visitor had spent a few days in the Valley; he had visited several potential suppliers; he was ready to return home and make his buying decisions. Getting that last sales pitch in was golden.

But I had a problem. As a new Vice President of Marketing at National Semiconductor, I knew I had to do dinner meetings. And I hated dinner meetings, for many reasons. First and most importantly, dinners took me away from my family. To get around this problem, I frequently suggested to visitors that they take time to freshen up at their hotel after a long day of meetings—"and I'll be happy to meet you for dinner later." Usually the visitor took the bait, enabling me to go home and see my wife and the boys before going out again to dine and court customers.

The other reason I hated business dinners was because alcohol—often lots of alcohol—was part of the ritual back then. Nothing was worse than sitting at a dinner and trying to make a technical point to a half-inebriated customer or prospect. This was a waste of time, and very unpleasant. I'm glad to see that at business dinners today, a glass or two of wine is the norm. In the span of 50 years, business leaders got smarter—and healthier.

To find an edge as well as to avoid the agony of business dinners, I started saying to customers who visited from out of town: "Let's do a breakfast meeting before you head home." Granted, executives today frequently do breakfast meetings. In the late '60s, they were practically unheard of. Some of my old colleagues have called me the "inventor" of the breakfast meeting in Silicon Valley. I'm not sure I should accept that claim to fame. But I do know that when I started doing breakfast meetings, no one else I knew of was doing them.

In any case, those breakfast meetings worked very well to bring in new customers. Generally, visitors felt good about making their final morning productive. They appreciated my willingness to come to their hotel early, before heading to the airport to fly back home. I got the last shot and often ended up getting the business.

And as I got accustomed to eating breakfast out, I started doing one-on-one breakfast meetings with members of my staff. I found that this was generally the best time to talk with people—when they and I are fresh and ready to start a new day. Breakfast meetings eventually replaced my luncheon meetings which I always found inconvenient because they interrupt a productive day.

There's also something special about a meeting over a meal. Conversation tends to be more open than in an office setting. People are usually more relaxed during mealtime. Sharing a meal helps enormously to build a relationship—and I believe it is an underused, undervalued asset in management. All that said, if you share a meal, think about doing it at a time that doesn't interfere with family time.

Do breakfast!

CHAPTER 9

Have Lunch

IN 1971, I WAS APPOINTED General Manager of the
Semiconductor division of National Semiconductor. Our headquarters
in Santa Clara, California, included marketing, engineering, finance,
and other corporate functions, but it was also our major wafer
fabrication site. Due to the labor intensity of the semiconductor
production processes back then, most of our 9,000 employees were in
manufacturing.

This was a big leap for me from overseeing about 100 sales and
marketing people. I had no experience managing manufacturing
operations, but I was fortunate to have an excellent staff of people
who were accomplished in that aspect of the business. That excellence
emanated from the top. National Semiconductor's CEO, Charlie Sporck,
was a manufacturing whiz.

I felt a huge weight of responsibility not only to learn the best practices
of manufacturing operations, but also to get to know the people in our
division. The traditional way to do that at National Semiconductor was
to invite employees to gather in some area of the plant and speak to the
crowd. Some employees would ask questions; the boss would answer as
best he could and then walk away with a sense of what the troops wanted
and felt frustrated about. This sort of employee "town hall" approach
struck me as a lousy way to get to know employees as individuals or to
build their loyalty and commitment to the company.

Working with our personnel department, I decided to start a series
of lunches with 20 or so employees from the plant. We decided to start
by inviting frontline employees who had the longest tenure at National

Semiconductor. I traveled often, but when I wasn't on the road or in the air visiting customers and our facilities around the world, I hosted these employee lunches once a week during my seven-year stint as GM of the division.

I learned more about our operations from those luncheons than from any other source. From the start, I adopted a policy of answering all questions with complete openness, explaining to the attendees that some of the material being shared could be considered company confidential but they were "in the family" and therefore trusted to keep the information confidential. I also stressed that there is no such thing as a "stupid question."

I learned that many of the employees in our plant were from foreign lands and that English was a second language. As a result, they didn't understand how American companies worked—and why we were structured as we were. I found that many of our U.S.-born employees were equally confused about how the American capitalist system worked. For instance, National Semiconductor was a very profitable company, but we didn't distribute any dividends to our shareholders; this concept of using retained earnings to invest for expansion was new to these employees. Back in those days, all National Semiconductor employees were shareholders, and they bought into the concept.

These plant employees wanted to do a good job, and they wanted our company to succeed. They were willing, even eager, to ask tough questions about work rules and procedures. I learned that many procedures that had been instituted by line management didn't make sense to the front-line workers—because they were in fact nonsensical. Some of these procedures were followed because "they said we had to do it this way" or "this is the way they always did it." I always instructed employees to find out who "they" are, and if they couldn't determine that, talk to me. I came away from these meetings with a real appreciation for our workers and with new ideas about how to make our manufacturing operations better.

Lesson learned: The strength of an organization is in the frontline people who have been in their jobs for some time. Giving these employees a say in the processes and procedures for building quality products is a great way to ensure product integrity. You can't know what your people are thinking if you don't meet with them in an environment that encourages input. Frequent lunches with up to 20 employees at a time lets you talk with a sample of your workforce in a very inexpensive way to ensure product quality and efficient manufacturing while increasing the commitment of the employee.

CHAPTER 10

Dress Down Fridays

TALK ABOUT AN AVALANCHE! A half century ago, corporate dress, even in Silicon Valley, was quite formal. Men in marketing, financial, and even engineering jobs wore ties and, if not suits, at least a sport coat and fine slacks in the office. The women in the office—generally assistants, which we called secretaries, back then—usually wore dresses. Slacks and a nice blouse were seen occasionally. This was just the way it was.

Summer presented a challenge dress-wise. Employees often had weekend plans to get away. As our staff would thin out on summer Friday afternoons, I asked around and found that many employees were going home to change clothes before heading out of town with their families.

To give people a break and try to keep them in the office a little longer in the summer, I implemented "Dress Down Fridays." Every Friday, from Memorial Day to Labor Day, no one was required to wear ties or dresses. Camping and vacation attire was perfectly acceptable. It worked. As long as people are neat, why insist on—or even expect—particular office apparel? Eventually our summertime Dress Down Friday expanded to Fridays year-round. Soon after that, managers tossed their ties, except when key customers came to visit.

I believe National Semiconductor launched the trend, and then dressing down quickly became the norm throughout the Valley. Silicon Valley set the trend for the rest of corporate America. That's a good thing. Allowing someone to dress the way he or she wishes is part and parcel of allowing people to bring their true selves to work. By the way, some of the sloppiest, worst dressed people I know have turned out the greatest work. You can't judge a tech genius—or a superstar in any industry—by appearance.

CHAPTER 11

Five Fingers

THOSE OF US WHO HAVE long been in the technology industry remember the old saying, "No one ever got fired for buying IBM." At National Advanced Systems (NAS), we faced the everyday challenge of trying to sell our mainframe computer systems against IBM. Big Blue, as IBM was known, commanded more than 80 percent of the mainframe market. In the U.S., Amdahl was also a major competitor;

in foreign markets, we competed against many other players. But pretty much everywhere, our greatest challenge was overcoming the perception that IBM was a safe bet and we were a risky alternative.

As I contemplated this dilemma, I tried to come up with ways to help our sales force overcome their perceived disadvantage. I constructed what I called the Five Finger Test. This was a test to evaluate our particular competitive challenge, but it could be applied to any situation where you have certain disadvantages vs. a competitor. In the Five Finger Test framework, each finger of the hand represents a different type of buyer:

• **The thumb** represents customers so loyal to Competitor X that they would buy from X even if X's price were higher than yours.

• **The index finger** represents customers that may be more price sensitive, but if they're presented comparable pricing, they would buy from Competitor X instead of your company.

• **The middle finger** represents customers that are neutral in their evaluation of your company and Competitor X.

• **The ring finger** represents customers that would buy from your company if all things were equal.

• **The pinky** represents accounts so loyal to your company that they would buy from you even if your price were higher than Competitor X's price.

In this Five Finger view of the competitive landscape, the first thing to acknowledge is that the group of customers represented by the middle finger is an empty set. I have yet to meet the totally unbiased customer. The neutral customer, I believe, doesn't exist.

Using the Five Finger Test at NAS was hugely helpful. We placed each of our customer prospects in one of the five categories, and then we assessed what we needed to do to sell to them more effectively. We had to be realistic—most of NAS's potential customers were categorized as thumbs: They would buy from IBM even if IBM cost more. Without some incentive, customers were not going to uproot their IBM systems and replace them with NAS systems.

It's never fun to compete on price, but we did some of that at NAS because we had to. We found that most customers would seriously consider buying our product instead of an IBM machine if we delivered the same value at 80 to 85 percent of IBM's price. The price difference was essentially the value of IBM's premium security.

The smarter way to respond to IBM's marketplace advantages was to make our machines better than IBM's. Back then in the early '80s (not so different from today), new applications were multiplying, and computing capacity requirements were increasing rapidly. NAS responded by designing products that provided 20 percent higher capability for the same cost as IBM.

The result? National Semiconductor didn't overtake IBM in the mainframe market, but we did manage to sell a lot of systems. And I learned valuable lessons about competing against a company perceived to be superior in the marketplace.

I applied those lessons several years later when I left National Semiconductor to go to Apple Computer. Even when Apple was a small company competing against entrenched giants, including IBM, it held that "pinky" position and could charge relatively high prices. Why? Because Apple, from its beginnings, built a valuable brand.

How do you measure brand value? The Five Finger Test offers an indicator: How much more value will a customer assign to your product than to a competitive product? If your product quality, pricing, and all other relevant things are equal, does your brand enable you to win a customer vs. your competitor? Can you command a higher price for your product or service? How much higher?

At the other end of the spectrum, if your brand isn't very strong, how much more revenue does your competitor command thanks to his superior brand value? What are you going to do about that?

If you find yourself in the "pinky" position of being a favored supplier even at a higher price, maintaining that relationship requires consistently excellent customer service and an "open kimono" approach. Give your customers an occasional roadmap of your future developments. Arrange for them to have appropriate executive contacts outside the sales organization. And regularly do a "Win Analysis" (Chapter 13) so you and everyone on the sales, marketing, and product development teams understand why the favored position is being bestowed upon your company.

And what if you find yourself competing against a superior brand that commands a premium price? Strategize to transition across the "fingers," one by one. Your first goal should be to move your most important prospective customers from the "thumb" (where they are exceedingly loyal to your competitor, regardless of pricing) to the "index finger" position, where they would consider buying from you at a comparable price.

I've found that moving a prospect from the first two fingers—the thumb and index finger—requires that you find some way to get your product into that customer's hands. Then you can build on the customer's good experience with your product. (A price concession on an evaluation product or a temporary installation on a purchased piece of major equipment has worked best for me. I advise against giving away anything for free. While sampling is a common practice in selling lower-cost products, items are not usually valued highly when they're not purchased.)

Once you get your product in the customer's hands, service is the key to loyalty. No matter what you're selling, the only true basis for a continuing business relationship is service. So, if your client has a preferred supplier other than your company, the best way to move in and get more business is to convince the customer to buy your product based on any plausible offer and then "out-service" the competition. This is hard work, but worth it. Strangely, favored suppliers frequently take their committed customers for granted and leave an opening for a service-oriented rival to get a foot in the door.

Lesson learned: Regularly perform a Five Finger analysis of both your current and potential customers. Then adjust your sales strategy and tactics accordingly.

CHAPTER 12

Customer Satisfaction Surveys

EVERY COMPANY IS IN the service business. If you're in business, you exist to serve your customers. That's a fundamental idea, as true for IBM and Apple Computer as it is for Joe's Hardware in your hometown. Okay, but how do you properly measure the level of service needed to maintain your customer's loyalty to you? It ain't easy.

Customer Satisfaction Surveys (CSS) are a common tool, but I have found them deficient in several important ways. For one thing, a customer's time is precious, so if you're surveying them, you're taking some of that precious commodity for a purpose that they likely view as unimportant. Even worse, if they resent that survey time, they might skew their answers negatively. But the bigger reason I don't like CSSs is that they rarely tell you what the customer really thinks.

For instance, if you're a relatively small vendor and your customer went out of the way to try out your product or service, that customer will likely rate you higher than the entrenched supplier. Why? To justify his own actions. That customer doesn't want his or her boss to see reports declaring that the entrenched competitor is superior because that would make the choice to try the small vendor look stupid.

We found this rationale to be true at National Advanced Systems, where most of our customers traditionally bought IBM machines and tried us out on an installation to see if we could live up to our sales pitch. They were taking a risk because turning against IBM in a major computer installation was downright job-endangering. In completing a CSS—which were widespread in the industry—it was not uncommon to complain about some aspect of IBM's offering because Big Blue deserved some "not for attribution" advice on how to treat its customers better. Meanwhile, customers who took a risk and tried NAS products gave us good scores in order to justify their decision-making to their bosses. While our favorable reviews came in handy in making sales presentations to new clients, I never believed that they were accurate.

I always knew that customer satisfaction of NAS skewed positive in these surveys. And if the survey results showed NAS equal to or below IBM's level of customer satisfaction (fortunately, a rarity), we had a real problem, and we had to act fast to fix it.

Another way to solicit feedback from customers is to set up a Customer Advisory Board. Many companies use these boards to get input on new product development. I found that this product development input consisted mainly of product features of competitors' equipment. While the input was interesting and gave us useful knowledge on where our product fell short, providing a feature that is already in the market will not help you get into the fast lane and pass your competitor. If you simply copy your competitor, you're committing to be the perpetual follower.

So, I found that Customer Advisory Boards told me what I already knew through market intelligence and didn't help us gain in our competitive ranking. I concluded that the best way to learn about what my key customers were doing was to visit their site and ask for a tour of their facilities. I could then see what hardware they were using and ask the "why" question. I learned far more walking through their shop than I did in any conference room. My experience, of course, was in the computer hardware business. This approach would not be as successful if I were a software purveyor.

Lesson learned: If you really want to build a relationship with your customers, visit them.

The best way to get your customer questions answered is to ask them when you're standing in the middle of their operations.

CHAPTER 13

Win Analysis

ONE DAY, EARLY ON in my role as president of National Semiconductor's National Advanced Systems unit, I was sitting in my office in Palo Alto, reviewing lost business reports from our field organization. My phone rang. It was a car salesman. I had just bought a new car, an Audi, after considering that and another vehicle. The man who was now on the line was the salesperson I had not purchased from.

I tried to be polite, but as the man quizzed me on why I had not purchased the car from him, my objective was to end the call quickly. I didn't want to answer his questions. I had made my choice, and that was that. Besides, I was busy.

When I finally got off the call, I turned back to my review of our lost business reports. Epiphany! It dawned on me that these reports might have been generated under circumstances like the one I had just experienced. What if the person collecting the information about our losses was similarly dealing with a prospective customer who just wanted the phone query to end? Pondering this made me wonder if the inputs on our lost business reports were reliable.

Right there and then, I had a second epiphany: We should find out why we win new business. This information could be even more valuable than why we lose pieces of business. I decided to institute a new procedure called "Win Analysis."

I knew that the salesforce would love "Win Analysis." Lost business reports often did not properly present the facts, and documenting losses was never a salesperson's favorite activity. Analyzing wins would surely be more energizing, and this practice could be key to developing important customer relationships.

I quickly got my direct reports in the NAS unit on board. We agreed that we needed to set some rules to impose discipline and rigor to this new process. One rule: While "superior salesmanship" could be cited, it couldn't be the only reason given for a successful close. Also, an adage of the selling business is "When you get the order, get out!" So, when the deal closes, our salespeople should not do Win Analysis on the spot. The rule would be that Win Analysis must begin after the salesperson seals the deal and within 72 hours of receiving the order for a new piece of business. Ideally, an executive of National Advanced Systems, rather than the salesperson, would initiate the Win Analysis process.

The first step of Win Analysis: The executive thanks the client for the new piece of business. This was particularly important at NAS because most buyers of our computers were moving away from IBM, the "safe" choice, to a relatively small supplier. The "thank you"—typically via a phone call—also demonstrated to the new client that management knew about the transaction and cared.

The second step of Win Analysis: Formulate a leading question to generate insights about why the customer bought our product. Such as: "Our computers are pretty complex systems with lots of features, and we constantly aim to focus on the truly important features that customers want. So, why did you buy from us?'" The feedback that we got was amazing. Practically every time, we learned something new about the customer evaluation process. By crafting our questions strategically, we learned what our customers told other people about why they bought from us.

Wouldn't you like to know what your customers tell your prospects? Win Analysis may hold the key.

I got the opportunity to do my own Win Analysis after one of my sales. In 1980, we won a contract to sell $8 million worth of computers to Electronic Data Systems (EDS). Ross Perot was the CEO of EDS, and Mort Meyerson was the President. Through the lengthy negotiations that led to the win, I had gotten to know Mort, and I had closed the order during a phone conversation with him. A couple of days after that call, I happened to be making a trip to New York, and I decided to stop in Dallas to do the Win Analysis with Mort in person.

Mort had joined EDS as a systems engineer trainee and rose quickly to President and Vice Chair of the company. At heart, he was a sales guy. And he was more than responsive to Win Analysis. Mort enthusiastically recognized the value of our process. After a few minutes of conversation about our new contract, Mort asked me if I would like to meet Mr. Perot. (Everyone referred to him as Mr. Perot.) To me, this was an exciting offer, and without pause, I said "Yes."

Mort and I walked down the hall to Mr. Perot's office. His office door bore a plaque that indicated his aggressive style of leadership: "Every good and excellent thing stands moment by moment on the razor's edge of danger and must be fought for." Ross Perot's office had an almost

New England look—rocking chairs, a Gilbert Stuart painting of George Washington, a Frederic Remington bronze on display, and lots of photos of his wife and five children.

I knew that I needed to leave in 45 minutes to catch my flight to New York City. No problem, I figured, since Mort said that this would be a five-minute meeting with Mr. Perot.

Well, we must have spent more than an hour together. And yes, meeting Ross Perot was well worth missing my flight. He was both kind and curious, asking me what had led me to the presidency of National Advanced Systems. I told him about working in the semiconductor industry and transitioning to computers.

"Those transistors are amazing: Tell me how they work," Perot said.

I had a way of explaining transistors—comparing them to the magnets that we played with as kids—and I got more technical as our conversation continued. Perot seemed impressed, perhaps even amazed by my knowledge.

I found his attention and his questions flattering but odd since his office was less than 10 miles from Texas Instruments. In 1954, TI had produced the world's first commercial silicon transistor and manufactured the first transistor radio. Did Ross Perot sincerely want to know how transistors work? Or was he quizzing me to see how my mind works?

I don't know the answer. But from our conversation, I knew that Ross Perot was much more than a transaction man. He placed tremendous value on relationships. My first meeting with Perot at EDS established a strong relationship that proved to be the foundation of our business well into the future. Our relationship started with an $8 million order, and Win Analysis helped make much more happen over the following years.

A couple of years after that first meeting at EDS, I received a call from Perot's office, informing me that he was considering an investment—$20 million, as I recall—in Steve Jobs' new company, Next. And he wanted to discuss the opportunity with me. We subsequently talked, and I encouraged him to make the investment. It was a good one, eventually producing a very nice return on investment for Perot, I was told.

Personal relationships are invaluable in business: They are often the key to long-term growth and success. A call expressing thanks for a new order is a good way to start a relationship that, over time, may bring unlimited value.

CHAPTER 14

The Planning Process

HAVING A BUSINESS PLAN is as fundamental to an enterprise as having desks and chairs. Developing the plan, however, can be a complicated process, with many twists and turns. During my tenure as President of National Advanced Systems, our business plan process encountered one such twist. I discovered that the people in our core management team didn't agree on what we were, what we wanted to be, and what precisely distinguished us from our key competitors.

One thing was crystal clear: This lack of common understanding of the core nature of our business was a problem. We agreed to work together to figure it out.

Step 1: What are we? The reality vs. the perception

First, we needed agreement on what we were, both real and perceived. This was critical because if we didn't know who we were, how could we possibly talk to our customers with clarity and properly provide them the products and services they needed? I assigned one of our best marketing people the task of asking both customers and a wide spectrum of employees (at the executive level and at the early managerial level) this question: "What do you consider National Advanced Systems to be?"

The survey results were fascinating. Both our customers and our own employees had widely divergent views of what NAS did. To use a spatial analogy, the answers were all over the map. That spatial analogy led us to realize that if we wanted to "get to San Francisco", we had better agree on whether we are starting from San Jose or Oakland or San Rafael.

That realization—that if you don't know where you are right now, it's almost impossible to map where you're going—gave us the foundation we needed to properly set a plan for National Advanced Systems. We developed a mapping process that enabled us to understand how we were unique vs. our competitors, to view our strengths without bravado, and most importantly to recognize and work on our weaknesses.

Step 2: What do we want to be?

The next step is to ask: "What do we want to be?" And specify the goals in your business plan. These goals typically include numerical targets, but they should also address certain aspects of the "what are we?" analysis that need attention. For instance, if the quality of your leadership is deficient, note that problem in Step 1, and then in Step 2, set a goal to fix it.

One caveat: In the most dynamic industries, such as technology, demand and supply of products and services change so quickly that market data often doesn't exist to help you assess whether your goals are realizable. That's OK. In your business plan, enumerate your dreams and aspirations over a reasonable time horizon.

Once audacious objectives are set, the organization can stretch its thinking to look for ways to make them happen.

Step 3: What's the plan?

OK, you're ready to finalize your plan. When the market shifts (you know it will!), or something goes wrong, you're grounded in an understanding of who you are, how you are perceived, and where you want to go. You have a plan, and you're ready to execute.

CHAPTER 15

Blinded by Sea Changes

ELECTRONIC TECHNOLOGY would never have advanced as quickly as it did if vacuum tubes didn't exist. The radio broadcasting, television, telephone, radar, computing, and recording industries owe considerable growth to the vacuum tube, which made these applications practical.

Solid state transistors became popular in the beginning of the semiconductor era and served the same function as vacuum tubes. In solid state technology based on the transistor, the electronic action of devices occurred in a solid state; in electronic equipment based on vacuum tubes, the electronic action occurred in a gaseous state. But these semiconductors didn't pose serious competition to vacuum tube electronics. They were used to power entirely new products, such as the mobile radio. The portable radio was a great new device, and everyone had to have one. To my knowledge, no one in the vacuum tube field felt particularly threatened by it.

As the 1950s ended, the possibility of combining multiple transistors in simple logic circuits was introduced just in time for the "race to

A model of the first single-chip calculator, 1972.
I still have this device, with its red LED display.

space" and specifically for the Apollo mission to put a man on the moon. Vacuum tube electronics weren't going to cut it in space applications. But again, these niche space and defense uses of transistors and microcircuits were not perceived as threatening to existing businesses.

That changed, of course. Today, transistors are ubiquitous. They have replaced vacuum tubes for most purposes. They're found in everything from household appliances to mobile phones, automobiles, and computers. Transistors have made devices smaller, cheaper, more efficient, more reliable, and more durable. And while no replacement technology is apparent, that shouldn't be a reason for complacency. Competition often comes from left field and without warning.

I recall being dispatched to Foxboro, Massachusetts shortly after I started at National Semiconductor. I had been assigned to evaluate what was happening at a company providing fluidic logic capability. One might chuckle today at the prospect of thinking that fluidics—or fluidic logic, the use of a fluid to perform analog or digital operations similar to those performed with electronics—could rival microcircuits. But that misses the point. Looking outside your direct product area to alternative developments and ways to do business is a must in the ever changing world of technology.

Perhaps no other segment of the global economy is as susceptible to fundamental shifts as the technology industry. Cathode ray tube displays gave way to liquid crystal displays (LCDs). Disc drives yielded to solid-state memory technology. And electronic communications to optical technology. As microelectronics have improved many aspects of our lives, there has also been collateral damage. Unable to recognize and adjust to impending sea changes, whole industries have been obliterated. In fact, I've witnessed two transitions where certain industries didn't know what hit them.

One was the calculator industry.

In the '60s, calculators were mechanical marvels that contained no

microelectronic parts. American manufacturers were, by and large, cool
to the idea of incorporating microelectronics. Their well-honed business
models were based on a "purchased bill of material" that amounted
to only a few percent of their total manufacturing cost. Why would
they mess with their sweet profit margins and innovate by using more
expensive microelectronic elements from the semiconductor industry?

Japanese manufacturers were less reluctant. Soon enough,
electronic calculators from Japan were flooding the American market.
Microelectronics became more and more sophisticated. Costs dropped.
And amidst the new investment and innovation, the calculator market
became highly competitive.

As we assessed our capability to put all the functions of a simple
calculator on a single silicon chip, I approached three leading American
calculator companies: Monroe Calculator in New Jersey, Addressograph-
Multigraph near Chicago, and Friden Calculator in San Leandro,
California. None of these companies were interested.

That disinterest marked a big mistake for these companies. The
transition to microelectronics, driven by the Japanese, buried them.
And the American calculator industry never recovered. The failure of
these U.S. managers to embrace change ended up costing thousands
of American jobs—and ultimately a chance to compete in an even
bigger industry than just calculators. Had those manufacturers
properly responded to market changes and innovated, they might
have been positioned to lead later on when calculators migrated into
microcomputers.

Companies often keep a keen eye on their direct competitors, and
rightly so. But these same companies will get blindsided and overrun if
they fail to look outside the box to understand the implications of new
technologies on their business and their products.

Don't get blindsided by sea changes. Watch the competition

vigilantly—not only your obvious rivals but new players that embrace new technologies with greater agility than you.

CHAPTER 16

Learn to Listen, Listen to Learn

IN BUSINESS MEETINGS of all types, some people talk too much. This can be a great positive! Particularly if you want to sell a product, a service, or an idea.

Here's what I mean: Surveys show that people tend to rate the quality of a meeting higher if they talked during the meeting. That is, people who talk during a meeting typically think it was a good meeting—even if others who did not talk during the meeting rate it mediocre. This implies that if you're trying to sell a product or a service or a big idea, the best thing to do is… LISTEN.

We've all been told that you can't learn anything while you're talking. That's obviously true, but the art of listening requires you to do much more than simply stop talking and prick up your ears. You need to get the other person talking. I'll share with you a few methods that have worked for me.

Let's start with a human resources example where an employee has done a really dumb and destructive thing. You're angry about what has happened and can't believe what your employee did. (I should point out that the example I'm going to give was first presented to me by a minister suggesting how to deal with a child in a correctional situation. The approach that the minister suggested has been effective for me in business environments.) Your first instinct is to ask, "Why did you do such a %&##@ thing?" This emotion-laced query can be a conversation stopper because it puts the employee firmly on the defensive, and it requires a lot of background information to explain why he or she behaved in an unacceptable way.

The question I suggest is: "What did you do?" While a person may not be able to explain the "why" of what he or she did, it's much easier to say "what" was done. Asking "what" instead of "why" also produces information that may shed vital new light on the situation and enable productive dialogue.

If you ask "what" was done and get silence in return, don't talk. Resist the urge to utter another word. Wait for the employee to speak. He or she will speak eventually. Don't let the employee change the subject. Stay on the "what" until you're satisfied that you have as full an explanation as you think you can get.

After the "what" question is answered to your satisfaction, the essential follow-up is: "Would you do it again?" If the employee realizes that the action was "dumb and destructive," your course of action, disciplinary or otherwise, will be different than if the answer is a defense of the deed. And if you discover that the employee did nothing wrong, apologize. Some people think an apology is a sign of weakness. I believe apologies show strength and confidence to get past the problem, clear the air, and move forward.

In a selling situation, the method to get another person talking takes a different form but is similar to the HR situation in certain ways. Let's start with what I call the "first call report." The first time you call on a new customer often determines whether you are ever going to succeed with that account. I suggest that you write a carefully researched "elevator pitch" to briefly explain why the customer will benefit from buying your product or service. And quickly turn the conversation to focus on the prospect and learn all about his or her needs. Ask questions like: What are your business issues? What is your purchasing procedure? What approval processes are needed for procurement?

Here's the key: These are all "what" questions. They seek facts, not opinions. If you sense reluctance to answer any of these questions, that's a good warning that their interest in doing business with you may not be as great as you hope. A company open to a new vendor typically will answer all the "what" questions.

If you're calling on a company that has its operations onsite and you're offered a tour, take it. If a tour isn't offered, ask if you might take one in the future. I've never gone on a plant tour that didn't teach me something about how to win business at that account. Moreover, while walking through a manufacturing operation, you can ask more "what" questions ("What did you do?... If it happened again, what would you do differently?... What is your new process?") and ideally open that door to new business.

Lesson learned: Listening is fundamental not only to learning. It is fundamental to leading successful meetings as well. Particularly meetings that involve firming up relationships with potential customers or other companies. Let the other person have the floor. Listen to learn what to expect from the new relationship and what you should do to build it.

CHAPTER 17

Risk Abroad:
The Stroke Of A Pen

*Speaking in Munich about how to design systems
using semiconductor technology*

LIKE MOST TECHNOLOGY companies, National Semiconductor chose to be an international company from its inception. We were competing with major companies in Europe and Asia, particularly Japan. Access to markets in countries that had their own semiconductor suppliers was always difficult. These countries typically erected barriers to "foreign" suppliers. Since we were competing in such a large and fast-growing market, this was particularly the case in the semiconductor market.

Australia was interesting to us in this regard. Australia represented a vibrant opportunity, particularly in telecommunications. Well-capitalized Australian companies were developing sophisticated systems for internal and international markets. These systems were loaded with semiconductor chips. To entice foreign companies to build semiconductors in Australia, its government placed high import tariffs on integrated circuit chips. For example, in the 1970s, a simple "gate element" logic circuit could be purchased in the open market for as little as 10 to 15 cents. The duty in Australia on these circuits was somewhat complicated to calculate, but it was around 30 percent plus a 25-cent minimum charge per device. So, a product that you could buy for less than 15 cents on the open market would cost about 45 cents in Australia.

We had an active market and a healthy business established in Australia. So, we took the opportunity to approach the government about opening a plant to assemble semiconductors in the country. While we couldn't manufacture products in Australia as inexpensively as we could at our largest facility back home in California or in one of our Southeast Asia plants, we could bring simple logic chips to market at 25 to 30 cents per chip and reap our normal profits. Producing other types of circuits carried various implications to our profit margins, but in the great scheme of this Australian opportunity, we could see the possibility of being almost a "sole source" for that market.

We proceeded to build and outfit a building in Bayswater, a suburb of Melbourne in southeastern Australia. One doesn't lay a cornerstone at a groundbreaking; one plants a tree. At least that's what I did. And it worked. Our market share skyrocketed. Yes, Australia was a relatively small market—at least compared to the U.S.—but telecommunications was an important market for us, and here we had an inside position.

But there were a lot of unhappy people. Competitors cried "foul" and lobbied Australia's government for lower tariffs. Even our local customers were not really happy with the tariff-heightened prices they were paying, so the government responded and made some minor adjustments.

The grumbling continued, though. And tariff policies became part of the debate in the upcoming election to choose representatives for Australia's legislative body, the equivalent of Congress in the U.S. We ended up losing—or the people who were defending our position ended up losing. Soon after the election, the rules changed and the effective duty on imported semiconductors was radically reduced, thereby enabling foreign suppliers to import their chips and sell them at a low price. Suddenly, our plant was no longer producing logic elements at a viable cost. We ended up closing the facility.

I learned from this experience in Australia a lesson that applies to any business in any part of the world: If an investment is safe only if some external rule or law is in place, be careful. You are probably in danger of losing your advantage. The Australian plant was a mistake because it brought to the country noncompetitive technology that could never compete in the global market. The stroke of a pen changed everything.

Another situation where similar factors were in play: In the late 1970s, I received a phone call from an engineer who said he and a small group of Jewish microprocessor designers were interested in joining National Semiconductor if we would consider opening a design facility in Israel. At that time, microprocessor designers were about as abundant as the proverbial hen's teeth. Here, I was being offered a package of half a dozen capable engineers who wanted to live in Israel. The opportunity intrigued me. We had a need for engineers on the ground in Israel.

Israel's government, it turned out, was quite interested in getting microprocessor technology capability going in the country. Country officials were very helpful as we considered what we wanted to do. The deal that the engineers were offering us was that they would join National immediately. National then had a year (as I recall) to firm up an arrangement and start building the design facility.

The failure of the Australian venture crossed my mind. But here we had real technology going to Israel. We had a team who wanted to live there. We also had a government that was accommodating, with the usual bureaucratic issues to work out.

We went ahead and hired the engineers. And we built the design facility. Jumping on that opportunity gave us an early foothold in an important technology market. Decades later, Benjamin Netanyahu told me that this facility was the first of its kind in Israel. The engineers chose to locate it in Herzliya, which today is a vibrant technology center.

This all worked because it was good for both parties. International development and expansion can't be based on political guarantees. The opportunity to plant a flag in a foreign market must make economic sense for everyone involved—and it must not be vulnerable to some political "stroke of a pen."

CHAPTER 18

Scotland is Burning: Crisis Management

IN THE EARLY 1970S, National Semiconductor established a wafer fabrication facility in Greenock, Scotland. The facility manufactured various types of wafers used in the fabrication of integrated circuits that were particularly important in our Digital Products line. The early 1970s had not been a robust growth period for digital circuits, but by 1977, demand was ramping up due to the birth of the personal computer and the dramatic advances of various types of electronics.

In April of 1977, I was in Florida, visiting customers and intending to spend the following weekend with friends who lived in Atlanta. Given these plans, my wife had joined me on the trip. On Friday, April 22, as Jean and I were getting ready to leave for Atlanta, I received a call from John Finch, my senior executive in charge of Integrated Circuit products.

"Are you sitting down?" he asked me.

When that question comes at the start of a conversation, you know the information to come isn't good. I assured John that I was sitting down. Then he told me that our Scotland plant had just burned to the ground.

This is not the kind of news I wanted to end my week of successful selling. Scotland was, at the time, producing more than half of all the silicon wafers that we needed to meet our digital products demand, as well as wafers needed for other National Semiconductor products. I knew that I had to go to Scotland immediately. As General Manager of the Semiconductor Products division, I was responsible for assessing the problems and determining what to do to recover.

As John and our senior team and I looked at our options, we realized that we had a trained workforce in Scotland, excess manufacturing capacity in our Santa Clara headquarters, and big demand for product. Meanwhile, the fire gave us a rare opportunity to reassess our commitment to Scotland as a manufacturing site. Greenock had been one of our most efficient, high-performing plants. We knew that we were going to have to start at near ground zero with a new facility.

Recognizing the talent that we had built up in Scotland, we decided within hours to rebuild the Greenock plant. Figuring out what to do with our hundreds of employees in Greenock was a bigger challenge. As I flew across the Atlantic, it was crystal clear to me that the most practical thing to do was to convince many of our Greenock personnel to come to America. These strong and dedicated Scottish workers could help us optimize our production capacity in Santa Clara.

About 24 hours later, our new plant manager, Jerry Brandeberry, met me at the airport in Prestwick, Scotland. It was a drizzly Sunday morning—2 a.m. due to my late flight arrival. Jerry had been in the job a mere three weeks. As he and I drove deserted roads 40 miles toward Greenock, we discussed our challenges so intensely that we didn't realize that we were driving on the wrong side of the road!

Nonetheless, we made it safely to Greenock. Fortunately, the approaching Monday was a plant holiday. This gave us plenty of time to devise a plan. Jerry said he would do all he could to help me lure the Scottish employees to California for work/training assignments. We would need at least 50% of Jerry's workforce to make the transfer plan work. In California, John Finch and Jim Smaha, who headed our Digital Products group, told me that they could use all the trained operators from Scotland that we could send to them.

As we developed this ambitious plan to transfer employees—most of whom had no passport and had never crossed the Atlantic—none of us had any idea whether it would work. Nothing like this had been done before. We were like pilots without a navigation system or even a map!

We aligned and collaborated and did the best we could. After we determined our internal plan, we scoped the complex details of our external plan. There were plenty of questions that we couldn't answer: How long would it take for the Scottish government to grant passports for our employees? How would we explain the situation to U.S. authorities so that they would let the Scots enter the country? How do we expedite reconstruction of a building that we did not own?

Suffice it to say, recovering from catastrophe requires asking questions and resolving a complexity of issues that you have never thought about, much less dealt with, before.

Crisis also brings out the best in people. And this crisis was no exception. Offers of help came from many quarters. Our largest competitor for digital products, Texas Instruments, had a plant in the south of England. TI offered to produce wafers for us. Amazing! While we didn't take TI up on its offer, I have never forgotten that generous gesture.

We did accept offers from governmental authorities on both sides of the Atlantic. The Scottish authorities arranged travel documents for our employees in record time. U.S. officials counseled the Scottish employees on what to say upon entering the U.S. so they would move through the process as smoothly as possible.

Meanwhile, the local Scottish authority that owned our burned building offered to sell it to us and transfer the insurance so we would be solely responsible for the rebuild. Other examples of support have faded from memory, but the lesson learned was clear: When you are in a crisis, open your ears and listen to the offers of help that are likely to come your way. You will gain a new appreciation for the kindness and generosity of people.

More than 70% of our Greenock workforce accepted the offer to move to California for 13 weeks to work in our plants there. The Scots arrived on Mother's Day, just three weeks after the fire. They performed magnificently. These Scottish employees proved to us that we had made the right decision to rebuild our plant back in their hometown. They would return home with a newfound appreciation for their work and reinforced loyalty to National Semiconductor. Some of these employees stayed in the U.S. for longer than the assigned 13 weeks. Some ended up immigrating to America.

The UK government also saw the entire venture as a win-win. When officials asked us to participate in "Invest in the UK" seminars to tell the story of our Scotland plant and the government's help in a time of crisis, we gladly stepped up.

By April 11, 1978, less than one year after the fire, we dedicated our new Greenock plant. The story of the fire and our recovery had swept throughout the British Isles. We had tried to get the Queen to come to our official opening, but for various reasons, that didn't happen. At a local restaurant, we hosted plenty of other people—including the plant's employees, along with their spouses—who had played pivotal roles in bringing the Greenock operation back to life. The party that night was one I shall never forget. The joy of seeing jobs return, a shiny new plant, and a future of being on the cutting edge of technology was overwhelming.

Crises reveal the best in people, particularly if you act like a good corporate citizen and contribute to the community. Excellent teamwork serves you as well as or better than any insurance policy that you might buy to protect yourself from an unexpected mishap.

CHAPTER 19

If You're Going to Take a Bath, Get Clean

STUFF HAPPENS AND things don't always go according to your plan. Your challenge may be a missed product delivery, a failure to win a piece of business, or a profit decline in your business. In any case, you have a problem you need to solve.

It's natural to try to solve problems by making minor course corrections. Addressing problems this way tends to be less disruptive and painful than making major revisions—or perhaps divulging the news that things are not going well. I've found that if a problem represents less than a 10 percent course correction, it might be possible to get away with a somewhat veiled set of actions that trim costs, staffing (perhaps by not replacing departing personnel), and spending on activities that are not considered critical.

But there are times when the trouble is larger, and you must make a major correction. This might mean you have to make a large reduction in force (a layoff), or reduce analyst expectations of your financial results, or announce a delayed product launch. My advice? If you're going to take a bath, be sure to get clean.

What does that mean? Looking first at the example of a reduction in force, these are no fun and shouldn't be fun. You are hurting the income and livelihoods of employees, and usually bosses have no idea what the full impact of a layoff will be on their families and future employment. It's natural for managers to want to wait as long as possible to pull the trigger and then cut the minimum number of people possible. This is almost always a mistake.

Why? I've never been involved in a reduction in force that, upon completion, was considered to have been done too early. Waiting to act when the company is in trouble is never a good idea. Furthermore, if there is anything worse for an organization than a layoff, it is another layoff six or eight weeks later when the boss realizes that the earlier cut didn't get at enough of the problem. An even worse situation is a third layoff a few months later. These subsequent layoffs are very hard on the people losing their jobs since people laid off in the first round had a head start in getting jobs that might have been available at other companies.

Cutting more deeply than you think may be necessary is the right thing to do. It's not the easy path, but it will assure the remaining staff that they are highly valued and needed to pull the business out of its rut. What if you cut too much? You hire. There is nothing like the lift an organization gets when it starts to grow and hire again. That first new hire—or rehire of someone you laid off—should be celebrated. Go ahead and signal your recovery to your employees.

And if you know that you're going to miss a product launch deadline or perhaps your "numbers" at the end of a quarter won't be so great, acknowledge the problem as soon as possible. Make an announcement that is closer to the lower end of your expectations than to the median. Then, do everything in your power to rally your troops and exceed the new expectations.

As I said, if you are going to take a bath, get clean. Recognizing and revealing the truth will earn you trust in the future.

WALKIN' ON WATER.....
IS JUST A MATTER OF SPEED!

CHAPTER 20

Frustration

FRUSTRATION GOES WITH being human. Most of us get frustrated with one thing or another. As I tried to become a more competent manager, I was concerned about how to deal with this issue— particularly the frustration of our employees.

One summer early in my management career, our family was at a Christian camp. While the camp filled the kids' days with lots of activities, we parents had time for relaxation and listening to speakers on various topics related to religion and family. One speaker said something

94

to the effect that "only frustrated people ever find real fulfillment." His statement hit me like a bombshell.

It became clear to me that our employees who never feel frustrated don't care as much about their work and the outcomes for their projects. They put in a day's work—and they may, in fact, do fine work. But nothing extraordinary results from their efforts. On the other hand, people who are trying to do some great new thing are frequently frustrated. The sources of frustration vary. They feel they don't have the right tools to get to a breakthrough, or they don't have proper support or access to certain people they perceive could help them. Or the last experiment didn't turn out exactly the way they had anticipated.

I decided to put to the test my newfound thinking about frustration leading to fulfillment. It was generally very well received. A typical situation would involve one of our engineers coming into my office to vent his frustration about something. I'd reply by saying something like "Terrific!" That, of course, would puzzle him—and in the moment, frustrate him further! I'd then go on to explain what I meant by "Terrific!" His frustration signaled to me that he's capable of great things and, most importantly, capable of fulfillment. Of course, every conversation was different—and as a manager, I worked to adjust thoughtfully to each situation. But typically I said something like this to the frustrated engineer: "It's clear that you care. You want to smash through a barrier. Being frustrated is a good sign."

Puzzlement usually turned to relief and an understanding that I truly wanted to help the engineer remove obstacles that got in the way of successful invention. Going back to that camp speaker, I came to understand that frustration may, in fact, be a very good thing. It may reveal a person's aspiration to do something great. And my job as a manager was to carefully coax that greatness and help them reach their audacious goals.

CHAPTER 21

The Centurion Effect

ONE OF THE MORE common questions I've been asked over the years is this: What are the biggest transitions that a CEO goes through, particularly if he or she works at both startups and large companies? Having personally experienced such transitions, I will tell you that the number of employees in a company tends to determine the greatest transitions.

I'm no expert on the Roman Legion, but I do know that soldiers were arranged in groups of 100 men, and the leader was called a "centurion." An effective centurion in business—that is, a boss who knows the skills and capabilities of 100 or more employees—is rare. As a company grows to 100 employees, most CEOs enter a zone of being out of touch with lower-level personnel. They rely on trusted direct reports to make sure people are doing their jobs as expected. Or if they are high control, they personally need to know what every single person does and oversee their actions. This kind of CEO usually fails.

The best CEOs of large companies rely on trusted direct reports and have a system to identify and get to know rising stars in the organization. Knowing select emerging superstars pays off in moments of challenge and change. Here are a few examples:

- **A problem arises at a remote site,** requiring the immediate dispatch of a trusted employee to sort out the issue. The CEO's direct staff can't leave their current responsibilities for any extended period of time. The CEO, knowing the emerging superstars in the organization, can, with confidence, send an appropriate fact finder or fixer. That assignment will in turn challenge the employee and help build his or her resume.

- **A key staff member falls ill or resigns** and must be replaced. CEOs without in-depth knowledge of personnel below the executive staff might look outside the company for a replacement. Great CEOs possess capability in the company—and know how to find it.

- A company wants to start a new division or acquire a new entity but doesn't have a lot of acquisition expertise. Assigning an employee to analyze and assess is always better than bringing in outside talent to do an analysis. The employee knows the company and its culture. Many acquisitions fail on cultural grounds, so having an existing staffer lead or at least contribute is a good idea.

Encouraging your staff to adopt a centurion mentality—to know your top 100 people and your best emerging talent—ensures that all periods of change, whether crisis or growth or retrenchment, are handled in the best long-term interests of the company.

CHAPTER 22

Tomorrow's Fish Wrap

TODAY'S PRESS IS tomorrow's fish wrap. Whether the press coverage you receive is good or bad, this is true.

Dealing with the good press, you must realize that we live in a flooded media world and the chance that all your customers see a favorable press piece is practically zero. To take advantage of good press, you must echo it. If you're to benefit from it, you must repeat the messaging to people who need to hear it.

This tactic to broadcast positive press has a lot of pluses: First, your good press is coming from a third party. You are not just putting out your own opinion. Rather, you're repeating what someone else has said. Getting the approval to spread good press is generally unnecessary if it's in a public source. If you sense that you should get approval, do so with the intent of confirming its accuracy. We all know that the press gets things wrong. You don't want your client quoted saying something that is going to be retracted tomorrow. And if you asked your customer to be quoted in a press release, make sure you have the release correct before sharing it publicly.

If you're contending with bad press, some of the same rules remain. Remember, not everyone saw the article. Don't be the source of your customer hearing about it. There are many ways of probing whether they know about the piece. If you get follow-up inquiries from other press outlets, you'll probably have to respond sooner or later. Try to do it later. Delay gives you a chance to see if the story has legs. If it doesn't, ignore it for now. There is so much media out there today that it's impossible to guess what will live past tomorrow.

My best advice for dealing with the press is to help them do their job. That generally requires you to understand their assignment. When you're called for a comment or interview, ask: Who is the intended audience? What aspect of the business is the article aiming to cover? What other companies or types of companies will be part of the story? What is the author's mission, and what points do they want to make? This last question is critical. If you're being interviewed for an article that is likely to favor or hurt someone, you need to know that. To the best of my ability, I've tried to stay away from stories that are hit pieces on someone or something. When excrement is being slung, it's likely to color everyone.

What do you send out when the news isn't good and you prefer to say nothing? My advice is to prepare a worksheet with three columns. In the first column, list your issues of concern. In the second column, list the truth about each issue. In the third column, note what you will say in your own press release. My rule is that everything in column 3 must appear in column 2. That is, what you say publicly must be the truth—but not necessarily all the facts. If you stick to this approach and don't say more until you know more of the truth, you will maintain your credibility. As you discover more truth, you can add that to Column 2— and, if you wish, to Column 3 and state it publicly.

This is an excellent method to maintain your credibility even when the press is not on your side.

CHAPTER 23

Picnic at the Plant

BACK IN THE '70s, it was customary to host an annual picnic for all employees. With 9,000 people in the Semiconductor division, the choices of where to go were pretty limited. For a couple of years, we gathered at Uvas Canyon County Park, a 1,147-acre nature park in upper Uvas Canyon on the eastern side of the Santa Cruz Mountains. It was a fair distance from our facility, so the turnout was not spectacular. Some 1,000 to 1,500 people, as I recall, showed up and enjoyed a day in the sun.

As we planned our next picnic, we wanted to improve participation as well as provide a good time for all our employees and their families. Our HR people had a good idea: Since National Semiconductor had just acquired undeveloped land next to its plant, they suggested we host the picnic right there at the plant. We could devise makeshift baseball fields, bring in entertainment for the young kids, and hire a band for the teenagers. Almost as an afterthought, we decided to do an open house so employees could show their families where they worked. Some of our staff volunteered to take turns operating equipment so the plant tours weren't sterile—rather, they were educational and even fun.

We figured that we would get a better turnout since, for sure, no one would get lost trying to find the location—they were going to their workplace. As that Saturday in June approached, there was quite a buzz among our employees about bringing their families to the picnic, but we still weren't sure about attendance. Well, 23,000 people showed up!

Our wild success that day, plus the good feeling that followed in the weeks and months after Picnic at the Plant, made me curious about why we had such a fantastic turnout. I made it a point, at every lunch and any other time I had the chance, to ask employees why they had come. As you might imagine, there were many reasons but, interestingly, the most common one I heard was that they wanted to show the people in their family where they worked and exactly what they did.

As I thought about this and probed further, it became clear to me why the employees were so eager to show off their workplace to family members. It related to my own experience with my dad, the carpenter. When I was a kid and we drove through the western part of San Francisco, he often pointed out buildings, mostly homes, that he had worked on. He was proud of what he had done. His work was visible; he could show his kids what he had accomplished.

In today's tech world, many jobs are difficult to understand and invisible to family and friends. While a century ago, you could walk down Main Street and see the occupations (the baker, the barber, the butcher, the cobbler, the dressmaker...) of a large segment of society, that isn't possible in many segments of today's economy. For instance, I would defy anyone to identify what is going on in the vast landscape of buildings across Silicon Valley. Those buildings all look similar. The work inside is not.

The Picnic at the Plant experience taught me a few things. First, managers can gain a lot of employee support by recognizing the family and including spouses and children in company activities.

Second, giving employees the opportunity to show off their work literally enhances the value of work. Let me explain: If dad or mom disappears every morning to "go to work" and the family has no real concept of what they do, it's hard to imagine how the children will learn to respect their parents based on their contribution to society. I grew up being proud of my dad and his contribution as a homebuilder. I think managers should help employees show off their work to their families and make their kids understand how, by coming to work every day, they do their part to make society better. This would enhance the value of work and the pride that children have for their working parents.

The more I thought about this, I realized that "hidden jobs" have quite a damaging effect. Going back to that "walk down Main Street" a century ago, children could readily identify what jobs were available to them as they grew older. With a large part of the job market invisible today, that job selection process is thwarted. We see this in college admissions: A huge percentage of students have an "undeclared" major. They don't know what they want to do, in part because they don't have a good feel for what job opportunities fit their interests and aptitudes.

I walked away from my Picnic at the Plant experience with a commitment to do all I could to enlighten employees' families about the contribution that they, as workers at our company, make to society. As often as I could, I opened our company to families so that our employees' children could understand not only the value of their parents' work but also the job opportunities that might open to them as they move toward careers of their own.

It may not be a picnic, but an open plant will serve your employees well.

CHAPTER 24

Speaking the Truth in Love...at Work

IN SILICON VALLEY tech companies, we had virtually no labor unions, so we could evaluate people for promotions without any constraints or rules set by an outside body. From the earliest days, the Valley was all about promoting on merit, but we were not always good at implementing that policy.

During one period at National Semiconductor when we were going through a "RIF" (reduction in force) of 10% to 15% of our employees, it came to my attention that many people who were getting laid off had been rated "above average" in their annual reviews. This pattern raised an obvious question: How could it be that we were laying off above-average employees when the total cut was supposed to top out at 15% of our workforce? In reviewing the matter with our HR people, I discovered that more than 90% of our employees had received "above-average" ratings.

Clearly, something was wrong with our annual review system.

What could or should be done to correct this situation—which, to me, had a number of ethical ramifications? The first ethical problem was that some employees had been led to believe they were doing an "above-average" job, yet were now, for the purposes of the RIF, being ranked in the bottom 10% of our workforce. That isn't fair—to quote an oft-used expression in employee relations. If an employee ranked at the bottom vs. his peers, he should know it.

The second ethical problem was that managers were not being honest.

They were leading employees into a false sense of security.

The third problem—and a significant problem for our company—was that employees who were already "above average" had no real incentive to increase their productivity and to perform better.

What to do? I went back to my Christian teaching and decided that in annual performance reviews, employees should be judged according to the biblical theme of "speaking the truth in love." The apostle Paul writes about this in the Book of Ephesians. His idea is that we should share difficult truths gently and kindly. As we all know, difficult things are best heard when our defenses are not up. Hard truths are more readily received in a loving, non-threatening environment. So, at National Semiconductor—as well as every other company I worked for—I strived to set a standard that we tell employees honestly and candidly and kindly how they performed.

CHAPTER 25

Diversity

MEANWHILE, LACK OF DIVERSITY of the workforce was never a major problem in Silicon Valley. There is a historical reason for this. In the 1960s and early 1970s, many technology-oriented college graduates were attracted to military or aerospace companies, or to businesses working for these sorts of government contractors. These jobs almost always required security clearances. Due to these clearance requirements, people who had immigrated to the United States from a foreign country couldn't easily get jobs in the aerospace or military industries. The exciting alternative was the semiconductor industry. We needed electrical engineers, physicists, chemical engineers, and more. The semiconductor industry was a wonderful melting pot of people from Europe, India, Vietnam, and other countries in Asia and the Middle East.

As many tech startups became multibillion-dollar companies and Silicon Valley grew up, so to speak, many of the immigrants started their own companies in the Valley. The cultural diversity blossomed and spread. That ethnic and cultural diversity remains an attractive feature of Silicon Valley executive leadership today.

Gender diversity in the factory was another matter back then in the 1970s. There were few women engineers, and the production line workers and assemblers were almost exclusively women. This frustrated me terribly. And as I tried to move women into management, I learned a sad truth. Most of the women didn't want supervisor positions; they preferred to work on the production line.

I needed to know why. Talking with our HR department, I got no satisfactory answers, so I brought the issue to the lunch table—my lunches with our frontline workers. When I asked 15 to 20 women whether they would rather work for a man or a woman, most said they would prefer a man. I asked the women how they expected us to promote more women into supervisor roles if they, the women on the line, made it difficult for them to succeed. They couldn't give me a good answer.

We had to work extra hard to help a woman succeed in a management position. And we knew we needed to be vigilant to make willing women "boss" because you can't run a successful business long-term if you tap only 50% of your workforce capacity. For any business to thrive, you need access to the full workforce capacity that is available. Because if you don't do that, your competitor surely will.

When I eventually left National Semiconductor for Apple Computer, gender diversity in management was not such an acute challenge. That's because Apple had a younger and more creative workforce than

National's. But no matter where you work, doing all that you can to make female managers successful is a critical part of any boss' talent development. Today, many more women than men are entering the professional workforce. In spring 2021, 59.5% of college graduates in the U.S. were women, and that gender gap is expected to grow wider. Women must succeed for your company to succeed.

CHAPTER 26

Changing Jobs

VIRTUALLY EVERYONE, at one time or another, finds themselves in a position to change jobs. The change might be within an existing organization or into a different company. Assessing whether a new job is going to "work out" is always stressful. In advising on this subject over the years, I've learned that there are many degrees of change involved in a job change. Understanding these types of changes can make a move less stressful.

First, when you change your job, you're likely going to be working with a new group of people you don't know—and people who do not know your talents and abilities. You're also probably changing the function you perform. Perhaps you've been working in the finance department but now you're moving into operations. Moreover, you need to learn new policies, procedures, and the right and wrong ways of the new corporate culture.

In advising job seekers, I suggest that they try to find employment where all three things—the job, the function, and the organization— are not changing all at once. But life and work are often out of our full control. So, what should you do if a lot of change is the only way you can go? If you know any of the people in the new job, that's a major positive. There's nothing better than a good personal relationship as you start a new position. If you don't have people you know and built-in relationships, make sure you know the job function you're being hired into and what the assignment entails. Your new boss and new colleagues will likely assume that you'll be ready to hit the ground running.

In the early days of your new gig, plan to spend up to 20% more time working than you're paid to do. Getting to know the company, the people, the job, and the industry takes time, but you will never be on a faster learning curve than during those first days. If someone offers to take you on a plant tour or to go to lunch to talk about the company, accept the invitations eagerly—and listen intently! Every company has its processes and lore; the sooner you learn both, the greater chance you'll have to successfully contribute and thrive.

CHAPTER 27

Opening the Japanese Market

FROM 1967, when I arrived at National Semiconductor, to 1984, when I joined the venture firm Kleiner Perkins Caufield and Byers, I traveled to Japan four times a year, and at least 60 times in total. During the early years, my goal was to sell semiconductors to the rapidly growing Japanese market and establish a manufacturing or marketing subsidiary. As the '70s ended, we were in a partnership with Hitachi to market IBM-compatible computer systems, and by the early '80s, when

I moved over to marketing at Apple, I was promoting Apple products.

Japan was never an easy place to sell products that were not made there. All sorts of Japanese government restrictions discouraged the import of foreign products.

The first time I carried semiconductors into Japan, I was advised not to use the words "transistor, electronic, or integrated circuit" at Customs. Since I knew no Japanese language, I could not understand the hubbub around me, but I'm convinced to this day that the Customs officials thought my product was some form of medical device. Amidst the bureaucratic stir, I managed to pass through the official airport clearance.

Given the attractive and fast-growing market, we were not going to give up too early in pursuing the Japanese, but visits to the Ministry of International Trade and Industry (MITI) were about as welcoming as the ones from their Customs officials. On my first visit to MITI, I was struck by the sight of some 20 dark-suited men seated at tightly spaced tiny desks in a small room with no partitions for privacy. On every desk was a stack of paper one or even two feet high.

We met with our designated official at his desk. He spent most of our meeting time showing me market data that suggested the Japanese market to be a fraction of the size we knew it to be. I visited MITI only one other time. It was clear that one of the jobs of these Japanese officials was to keep us out of their market.

We came up with an alternate plan. At the time, the island of Okinawa, Japan's fifth largest island, was still controlled by the United States—a relic of the settlement after the Allied victory in World War II. Okinawa was scheduled to revert to Japan in the near term, and we learned that once the reversion took place, all plants on Okinawa would continue to operate. This knowledge gave us the idea to buy a plant on Okinawa. We then agreed to shut the plant down in favor of a design and applications lab on Honshu, Japan's main and most populous island.

Since Japan was a leading manufacturer of consumer products, having a design facility on the country's most populous island, which includes Tokyo and other large cities, was essential.

The scheme worked but there were other issues. The Japanese grossly undervalued their currency. This was obvious even to consumers: The price of Japanese products in the United States was far below prices for comparable products in Japan. But Japan was dedicated to an "export policy." President Nixon rescinded the existing 360 yen to U.S. dollar exchange rate. There was outrage, but the rate settled at about 240 yen to the dollar for a few years. That was better but not low enough to match reality. In recent years, the rate has been around 100 yen to the dollar, which is much closer to reality.

The Japanese were tough competitors throughout the 1970s. Today, China dominates the conversation about the fairness of trade practices. If you take news articles from the 1970s and do a "search and replace" of the word "Japan" with "China," you could practically publish it today. The players may change, but the tactics of war remain the same.

Thanks to our taking a number of important steps, the U.S. ended up beating the Japanese in the semiconductor market. In order of importance, these steps enabled American leadership:

1. **Fixing the "dumping" problem** by adjusting the trade imbalance caused largely by currency manipulation.

2. **Innovating.** U.S. suppliers moved to market quickly with new chip designs. The Japanese had a difficult time keeping up with our pace of invention. Japan lacked the essential entrepreneurial spirit.

3. **Aggressively marketing and selling our products in Japan.** The Japanese were active in our market; we had to make sure they saw us in Japan.

4. **Competing globally.** We aimed to be in as many international markets as we could justify financially. In markets where U.S. suppliers were not active, the Japanese did very well. They understood how market

dynamics vary around the world. In computer systems, for example, the Japanese used Australia as a market to improve their strategies and tactics in English-speaking countries.

Today, China is considered the nemesis in semiconductors and in other industries. My belief is that we could improve the competitive position of American suppliers if we took many of the same steps we took vis-a-vis Japan 50 years ago.

CHAPTER 28

Partnership

BY THE LATE 1970s, National Semiconductor had succeeded in the business of producing and selling grocery store point-of-sale systems, the technology behind automated checkout counters. It was around 1978 that the company decided to enter the mainframe computer business. The economics of selling these powerful and expensive machines were terrific, with prospective profit margins almost too good to be true. We formed National Advanced Systems (NAS) to build our presence in this lucrative market. After heading the semiconductor business for seven years, I was asked to serve as President of this new subsidiary.

At that time, the IBM System/370 Model 158, a medium-sized high-performance data processing system, was selling for more than $2 million. We estimated that IBM's cost to manufacture that machine was about $95,000. We believed that we could, using National Semiconductor's own integrated circuit supply, duplicate IBM's performance with a machine costing $150,000 to produce, and we could sell it for $1.5 million. It seemed like an easy way to coin money.

We had a marketing partner in Itel Corporation, which was already marketing our memory add-on systems to supply memory additions to IBM products. Itel was eager to enter the IBM "plug compatible" business, and we were ready to supply the market. Meanwhile, Itel had a marketing relationship with Hitachi and a marketing arrangement to lease IBM systems. A National Semiconductor-Itel partnership looked to us like an ideal way to compete in this important new sector.

We shipped our first systems in 1978 and we felt encouraged. In our first year selling mainframes, we generated more than $100 million in revenue and put $40 million of that on the bottom line. But Itel's sales of our mainframe computers quickly started falling off. Inventory of our machines was building up in their warehouse. Soon after, Itel declared its departure from the plug-compatible market and asked us if we would buy that piece of their company. Such an acquisition would make National Semiconductor a fully integrated computer supplier with capability to sell, service, market, and produce computers—and carry the big costs of all those operations.

There was another problem with this prospective acquisition. Itel sold high-end Hitachi products. National did not have a warm relationship with Hitachi. In order to make any sort of deal succeed, National needed to have a healthy relationship with Hitachi. This was my problem to solve.

I agreed to travel to Japan to try to secure the rights to sell Hitachi machines and build a relationship with Hitachi's leaders. I did not have an invitation to meet anyone; I'd be going "hat in hand" to try to resolve our issue. The Itel people tried to help, but they were unsuccessful in setting up any meetings.

I sat in my Tokyo hotel room for a full week, waiting for a meeting. This may sound crazy that I had to sit in one place and wait for an invitation to come in. But keep in mind, this was long before mobile phones. So, I sat and sat and sat and stared at the ceiling of my hotel room. It was not fun. And I was under intense pressure to deliver for the bosses back at National Semiconductor headquarters in California.

Making the challenge even more difficult, National was, at the time, considered an anti-Japanese company. Charlie Sporck, National's CEO, said I, among all our senior executives, had the best ability to smooth relations. Other executives in our company were more aggressive than me—and certainly more effective than I would ever be in certain situations. For this assignment in Tokyo, however, everyone knew that aggression was not going to be the solution.

I was terribly disappointed and distressed when, after seven days stuck in that hotel room, I concluded that a meeting was not going to happen. I got on a plane and returned home. But the struggle wasn't over yet. A few months later, an Itel executive named Tommy Tan, who had a strong relationship with the Hitachi people, broke the ice and secured a meeting for me.

So off I went to Japan again—this time with an appointment. As it turned out, Hitachi had a problem similar to ours. Like us, Hitachi had no sales and marketing capabilities in house. The prospect that National was about to buy Itel, Hitachi's marketing partner, was an ominous one, given our tense relationship. This created an opportunity for us.

How did we end up with a successful National Semiconductor-Hitachi partnership? First, we recognized that our mutual need—to sell high-end computer systems—had to trump our personal animosities. Moreover, if a partnership was going to grow and help the bottom lines of both Hitachi and National Semiconductor, there had to be assurance that the sales and marketing arm was going to vigorously support both manufacturing businesses.

That mutual understanding led to resolution. After we acquired the Itel business and started selling large computer systems for Hitachi, we not only fulfilled our commitment to sell 30 Hitachi machines; we sold 31 machines! We developed a positive working relationship with Hitachi that later paid

Articles explaining how to use semiconductors to design advanced technology products proliferated in the 1970s. Ordinateurs is the French word for computers.

even greater benefits. National successfully exited the large machine business by selling our operation to Hitachi. Performance to promise and careful adherence to building personal relationships made that happen. But only after there was a clear need identified on both sides of the table.

I walked away from that experience with a new understanding that "need" for both parties is the best way—and usually the only way—to form a successful partnership

And the best partnerships are built on trust. Over the years, as our partnership with Hitachi grew and flourished, our contracts became much simpler. In fact, our contracts frequently were simple one-page documents with pricing and a few other essential points. I recall one day when we were renewing our deal with Hitachi, and the two companies' lawyers were disagreeing with each other. I was in the boardroom with the attorneys and Mr. Tanaka, my counterpart at Hitachi. Mr. Tanaka said to his lawyer, "You work for me, right?"

"Yes, sir," the attorney replied.

Motioning to my lawyer, Mr. Tanaka said, "And he works for Kvamme-san, right?"

"Right," the Hitachi lawyer responded.

"We agree. Now you two agree!" Mr. Tanaka said.

With that directive, the problems that the two lawyers were having suddenly evaporated.

You really cannot underestimate the value of strong personal relationships in business. In this situation, I had the advantage of negotiating with a good man at Hitachi, Mr. Tanaka. While the attorneys complicated things, Mr. Tanaka, a truly nice guy with a good sense of humor, was determined to keep it simple. He and I came together because we saw one another as real people and we decided to trust each other.

After we renewed that contract with Hitachi, I took my wife and our son Damon with me on one of my many trips back to Japan. Mr. Tanaka hosted us. After the trip, Damon made a Japanese tea service, a tea kettle and cups, in his pottery class. He engraved the kettle with Mr. Tanaka's name in Japanese characters. When I gave the tea service to Mr. Tanaka, he was deeply touched.

CHAPTER 29

Traveling to Japan

I'VE TOLD YOU ABOUT the reluctance of Japanese government officials to make travel into Japan easy for foreigners. This following story is an example of that—with a humorous conclusion.

In the early 1980s, the relationship between National Semiconductor and Hitachi was quite good. National Advanced Systems was performing to expectations on the computer systems that Hitachi was supplying. And personal relationships between the two companies had improved dramatically since the early days.

The semiconductor divisions of the two companies wanted to explore the possibilities of doing more together. A good first step, we agreed, would be for National Semiconductor's CEO, Charlie Sporck, to visit Hitachi's semiconductor chief and his team in Japan. I arranged for Charlie to go to Tokyo on his way back from a trip to National's facilities in Southeast Asia. Charlie suggested—and Hitachi agreed—that he would bring along Dr. Ed Ross, one of National's executives from its semiconductor operations. The plan: Ed and I would fly to Tokyo one day before Charlie was to arrive from Hong Kong, where he was wrapping up his Asia tour.

Ed had never been to Tokyo and was excited to see the beautiful

Japanese capital. As planned, Ed and I flew to Tokyo one day ahead of Charlie's scheduled arrival. As soon as we landed, we discovered that meeting Charlie would be complicated. International flights were landing at a different airport: a new airport in Narita that was very controversial. Local farmers had objected to the airport's construction and were protesting. We knew that the trip to Narita would be a hassle—an hour-plus train ride. Nonetheless, we would do what we had to do to meet Charlie. At least we could spend our time on the train discussing our Hitachi meeting scheduled for the following day.

Upon arrival at Narita, we landed in a long line of people wanting to enter the airport grounds. This heightened security was related to the controversy and the farmers' protests. After a considerable delay, we reached the desk where an officer was stationed to waive us into the airport. But not quite yet. We had to show our passports. And Ed had left his passport at our hotel in Tokyo.

The officer asked us to step out of the line and into a holding area. Ed explained that his passport was back at the hotel. He tried to convince the officer that a call to the hotel could resolve the problem; the hotel would send someone to his room, Ed said, and they would confirm that his passport was exactly where he said it was.

The officer would have none of it. No passport = no entry. I started making jokes—painting pictures for Ed of potential crazy consequences of him traveling in Japan without his passport in his possession. I was chuckling. Ed was not.

Clearly wanting us out of his holding area, the officer finally told us that we would be taken to airport police headquarters to determine our fate. A police van whisked us away to a nondescript building that appeared to be some sort of police facility. As we entered and ascended a set of stairs, I continued to "advise" Ed of the consequences of his fate. These comments elicited chuckles from me and groans from Ed.

We finally arrived at a counter in a room with one officer in sight. He gave each of us a form to fill out, with personal questions about our trip—why we were in Japan, why we were in Narita, how long we planned to stay. Thinking that we might never get out of this place, I was tempted to jot down joke answers. The officer was deadpan serious. My lame attempts at comedy stopped. This was getting serious.

The officer took our two completed forms and walked across the room to study them. After reviewing my paper, he seemed satisfied. Of course, I was not the problem because I had my passport with me. The officer then turned to Ed's form. After a brief scan, he walked back across the room, clearly agitated. Pointing to an item on Ed's completed form, he indicated that he wanted an explanation of that entry. Mind you, he didn't speak English, but it was obvious that it contained something he didn't like.

Right then, Ed turned to me and said, "I really was born on December 7, 1941!"

December 7, 1941, is the date that the Japanese attacked Pearl Harbor. The Japanese killed 2,403 U.S. personnel, including 68 civilians, on that day of infamy—which led to American counterattacks and ultimately an Allied victory against Japan and Germany. How crazy was it that Ed was born on Pearl Harbor Day? He was just being honest. He had to list that as his birthday, but his honesty did not go over well.

And at this point, I was thinking that we might be spending the night in a Japanese jail!

Fortunately, the officer, upon Ed's confirmation of the accuracy of his birthday entry, decided to let us go. We went to meet Charlie—yes, a little late. He got a big kick out of our story. And yes, after that brush with the Japanese authorities, we carried our passports wherever we went.

As I said, I have traveled to Japan more than 60 times. If I've learned anything about the country, it's that the Japanese take their bureaucracy very seriously.

Pioneers

GOING WAY BACK to its roots in developing the first semiconductors in the 1950s, Silicon Valley has attracted extraordinarily smart and creative people with all sorts of personalities and work styles. I had the great pleasure of working with some of the most interesting and important folks in the Valley. I will discuss just four of them here. All are now deceased. All of these brilliant men helped make the Valley the remarkable, innovative, world-changing place it is today. And I hold **Bob Noyce, Bob Widlar, Jack Tramiel, and Steve Jobs** in high regard for their contributions.

CHAPTER 30

Bob Noyce

WHEN I JOINED General Electric's Semiconductor Products Division in Syracuse in the fall of 1960, GE had a full line of transistors for use in consumer, industrial, and some military applications. I was assigned to the test and measurement department. Our job was to characterize transistors and some early integrated circuits for use by customers.

One of our best-selling transistors was a germanium alloy unit that was popular with a wide variety of customers building digital systems. One of its troubling characteristics, however, was that when the input signal instructed the transistor to "turn off," there was a long delay, called storage time, before the output responded to the signal.

Going to class at night, I had simultaneously started pursuing my MSE (Master of Science in Engineering) degree, with a focus on semiconductors, at Syracuse University. One of my first courses covered switching characteristics of transistors and the importance of the recombination properties in the semiconductor chip to reduce storage time. This coincidence of studying recombination at school and struggling with storage time at work was fortuitous.

My study informed my work at GE. The company was using finely polished germanium pellets to build alloy junction transistors. The polished surface enabled good emitter and collector alloys to form the device, but I reasoned that it eliminated recombination sites. I suggested that we do something to rough up the surface after the alloy steps. We had the capability to "sandblast," so we tried that. It worked wonders. Storage times decreased dramatically. I was a young hero. Even the General Manager of the division, Dr. Len Meyer, took note. And, while we were not "buddies" by any stretch of the imagination, Dr. Meyer kept his eye on me for the remaining time I was in Syracuse.

It was through Len that I first heard the name Bob Noyce.

I'm not sure how Len knew Bob. A physicist by training, Noyce had co-founded Fairchild Semiconductor in 1957 and invented the monolithic integrated circuit two years later. The monolithic IC chip put all components on a chip of silicon and connected them with aluminum lines—an innovation that fueled the computer revolution. Len was very excited that he was going to see Bob Noyce at an upcoming conference. Why Len told me, a young engineer buried deep in the organization, about his regard for Noyce is something I no longer remember. But it affected me and made me hope to meet Bob Noyce someday. I had so much respect for Len that anyone he held in high regard must be a great person.

Testimony of

E. FLOYD KVAMME

before the

U.S. SENATE BUDGET COMMITTEE

January 26, 1981

I would like to thank you, Senator Chiles, for this opportunity to address your Subcommittee on the critical question of industry growth and productivity.

My name is E. Floyd Kvamme; I am a corporate Vice President of National Semiconductor Corporation, formerly General Manager of its Semi Division, and now President of the National Advanced Systems Corporation, a wholly-owned subsidiary of National Semiconductor, engaged in the manufacture and marketing of large-scale computer systems. I am appearing today on behalf of the Semi Industry Association.

The semiconductor industry has established a track record of high, profitable growth; of worldwide competitiveness in an ever-widening array of market applications; and of continuing productivity improvement.

We now, however, find ourselves facing a new problem in both domestic and international markets. That problem is that the business environment and government practice of the United States are not competitive with those of the home environments of our trade competitors. It is true that trade barriers have in fact come down and, by and large, our industries are competing directly, head to head, in a world market with foreign industries. But those foreign industries are increasingly supported by their governments and by the structure of their economies. This is especially true of our main competitors in Europe and Japan.

There is not equality in terms of market access; there is not equality in terms of access to capital and cost of capital. There is not equality in terms of available human resources. That is what I am here to talk about today.

First, are semiconductors really so important?

Semiconductor technology has been labeled the crude oil of the '80's because it will fuel all segments of the $100 billion world electronics industry - including computers, telecommunications, instrumentation robotics, consumer and defense sectors. The industry will grow at a 15-percent compound annual growth rate during the '80's.

Our basic industries - such as steel and autos - are using semiconductor-based technology to modernize their production processes, improving productivity and regaining international competitiveness.

The U.S.-Japan rivalry
hit its peak in the early '80s.
I testified about the
semiconductor industry
before the U.S. Senate
Budget Committee.

In 1981, Fortune called National Semiconductor "the streetfighter of Silicon Valley" and noted that the company "moves with lethal speed to slash prices, gobble up market share, and drive competitors from the field." The guy holding the wafers is CEO Charlie Sporck.

When I left GE for Space Technology Laboratories and worked on Fairchild devices, my respect for Bob Noyce was a key reason I changed jobs again—to join Fairchild Semiconductor.

Starting at Fairchild in 1963, when I was assigned to work with large customers that wanted custom-designed products, Bob Noyce sometimes was part of the customer meetings. While most meetings took place at the plant, some required visits to customer sites. I remember one visit to Scientific Data Systems, a mid-range computer company in Los Angeles. Bob and I flew down to meet with SDS's President, a well-known tech entrepreneur named Max Palevsky. I'm not sure that Bob and Mr. Palevsky had met prior to that meeting, but they seemed to hit it off well. While Palevsky, clearly nervous and excited to work with us, continuously circled our conference room table as we talked, Bob showed his salesmanship by assuring our commitment to SDS's product. Bob was being sincere; he understood that our performance would make or break the SDS design. If we didn't deliver, their program would fail.

We performed well on the project. A few years later, when Bob and Gordon Moore left Fairchild to start Intel, Max Palevsky became a founding investor and Intel board member. I believe Palevsky's confidence in Bob's capability started at that early meeting. That was only one of several meetings where I saw Bob in action, but I left each one respecting his style in taking responsibility for the needs of customers.

A couple of years after Intel was formed, I got a call from Bob, asking me to come over to his house to talk about business. I suspected he had an opening that he wanted me to fill. I was right. Bob offered me a key job running Intel's marketing organization. At that time, I was committed to National Semiconductor and its leader, Charlie Sporck. So, I didn't accept Bob's invitation. Nonetheless, being offered a high-level job by someone of Bob's stature—arguably the leader of Silicon Valley—was a thrill.

We had a few more encounters during the 1970s until later that decade when the industry was threatened by the incursion of Japanese manufacturers to the semiconductor market. Japan's trade practices were not helping the situation, and Silicon Valley had scant political clout in Washington. I was on the board of the Western Electronic Manufacturers Association (later known as the American Electronics Association (AeA) and now called TechAmerica) and had agreed to be the keynote speaker at the group's annual event in Palo Alto. It was there, in the Cabana Hotel amidst a crowd of 200 people, that Bob Noyce, Charlie Sporck, and a couple other members of the Valley's semiconductor leadership pulled me aside and said they thought this meeting would be an ideal time to "throw down the gauntlet" and "declare war" (or words to that effect) on the "Japanese problem."

They asked me to modify my speech—which was supposed to be a mild-mannered update on industry activities—and strongly express our concerns about the Japanese threat. I agreed. As the dinner proceeded, I read and reread the speech I had written and penciled in the tough language they had suggested. I was increasingly nervous and even dreading walking to the podium. Finally, the moment came to get on stage and make my remarks.

As the bosses ordered, I talked tough and called for, among various other penalties, a boycott of Japanese semiconductors.

Saying those strong words aloud made my heart skip a few beats. Right in front of me, as I spoke, I saw a full table of members of the Japanese semiconductor industry. They had apparently flown to California to be part of this important conference and expected to be welcomed—if not warmly, at least politely. As I spoke, the Japanese executives, in one coordinated unit, stood up from their table, walked to the back of the room, and exited the meeting. Never before, nor since, has one of my speeches had that effect.

It was not fun or pleasant at the time. But as I look back on the experience today, I think Bob and Charlie and the other members of the industry who encouraged me to make those harsh remarks were right. We had a problem that needed to be addressed, and talking about it candidly and publicly was a first step.

By the late 1980s, Japan controlled almost 50% of the global semiconductor market. And Japan's government was playing a major role in funding the development of semiconductor technology. In 1987, the Semiconductor Industry Association responded by working with Washington to create Sematech, a government/academia/industry consortium to advance U.S. competitiveness—much like the Japanese Ministry of International Trade and Industry served Japan. Called a "technological catalyst," Sematech was dedicated to "fundamental change in manufacturing technology and the domestic infrastructure to provide United States semiconductor companies the capability to be world-class suppliers." Early participants included 31 universities and companies such as AT&T, IBM, Intel, Hewlett-Packard, and Texas Instruments, as well as National Semiconductor.

Bob Noyce and Charlie Sporck played vital roles in establishing Sematech, which powerfully advanced American technology and effectively beat back Japan's unfair practices. Sematech, I believe, saved the American semiconductor industry.

Bob made the ultimate sacrifice, leaving his leadership role at Intel to head Sematech in Austin, Texas, at its start. Bob's dedication to advancing the American semiconductor industry could not have been more strongly demonstrated than by that act of dedication. I once heard him say that the only real benefit of living in Austin was that his flight from there to his favorite ski area in Aspen was 10 minutes shorter than it was from San Jose—not much of a perk.

I last saw Bob in 1990 a few weeks before his death. He was trying to help with a semiconductor company that Kleiner Perkins had invested in. As always, his concerns were for the semiconductor industry—that we do all we can in America to stay in the forefront of semiconductor technology.

Bob Noyce was a true stalwart in making Silicon Valley the amazing place it is today. I'm happy to have had opportunities to work with him.

CHAPTER 31

Bob Widlar

BOB WIDLAR CAME to the Valley in 1963 and joined Fairchild
Semiconductor as a design engineer in John Hulme's Applications
Engineering group. He came from Ball Brothers Research in Colorado,
where he developed analog and digital equipment for NASA. We knew
almost immediately that Bob was different.

Bob had his own set of support personnel headed by a technician
named Mineo Yamatake. Bob kept pretty much to himself. He didn't
care for meetings. He seemed to simply want to do his job, which was to
design analog integrated circuits.

His first major product was the first volume-selling operational
amplifier, the uA709. It was a huge hit for Fairchild and a high-margin
product that drew envy across the industry. The uA709 cost about five
dollars to manufacture and sold for about 60 dollars.

Bob was an eccentric engineer with an artist's mindset. When you
talked with him about circuit design, you realized that he thought of the
circuit differently from the way other designers did. The conventional
way to think about integrated circuits involved transistors, resistors,
capacitors—the components of a circuit design. Bob, in contrast,
thought about how the circuit was made from a silicon wafer viewpoint.

I called him "the sculptor in silicon." In those days, circuits typically
were made by using photolithography, which involved cutting film
material (called rubylith) to the pattern of each layer of the circuit. If
you looked at the chips that Bob designed, it was difficult to figure out
where the various components were. He hid some below bond pads, and
others in other parts of the chip that were not obvious. Rather than use

a draftsman to prepare the photo-masks for manufacturing, Bob used a razor blade to "design" his own photo-masks. No one was to know the details of Bob's design.

He was a genius.

And as he became better known across the technology industry, Bob was taken to industry conferences to introduce his designs. In Stockholm, we had customers paying to come to our sales conference—that's right, paying to sit and hear National's sales pitches—because Bob Widlar was on the agenda. We had 900 people there, and 1,000 people at our semiconductor seminar in Paris. Tragically, Bob couldn't control his drinking problem. After lunch, he typically was so sloshed and thick-tongued at these events that I would have to translate for the translator. The translator assigned to interpret the English-language speeches for the international audience sometimes had no clue what Bob was saying—or slurring.

Bob stayed at Fairchild for just a couple of years. After the enormous success of his first products, he wanted to be in a company where his compensation was more closely tied to the economic value of his output. He and Dave Talbert, the head of the manufacturing division that produced Bob's circuits, quit Fairchild to go to tiny National Semiconductor in 1966.

Fairchild required every departing employee to fill out a five-page document indicating why he or she was departing. Of course, Bob opted not to fill out the form the way other people do. Rather, he scrawled five words—one word on each of the five pages:

"I

Want

To

Get

Rich."

Bob and Dave moved into a little building in Santa Clara that National Semiconductor, which was headquartered in Danbury, Connecticut, had

The I.C.

get smarter, invent better and be
one-up on practically everybody

Seminar.

WIDLAR
Great Linear Guru

KVAMME
Wizard of MOS

In case you missed these two brilliant gents last year in Paris, we've got them together again for a seminar on what's happening with Linear and MOS. Bob Widlar, who designed more than half the world's linear circuits, will pursue needed ideas and inventive applications. Floyd Kvamme, who has answers to micro-circuit questions that nobody's even thought of yet, will eloquently reveal some new *how to do it* wisdom on MOS. We've booked them into *the Century Plaza, Los Angeles, on June 18, 1968.* We ran out of chairs in Paris, so better reserve one instantly.

Besides lunch you get all this for $15.

9:00– 9:30	CIRCUITS AVAILABLE TODAY	*Kvamme*
9:30–11:00	VOLTAGE REGULATORS	*Widlar*
11:00–12:00	MOS IN MEMORY APPLICATIONS	*Kvamme*
1:00– 2:30	OP AMPS & VOLTAGE COMPARATORS	*Widlar*
2:30– 3:00	MOS ANALOG SWITCH APPLICATIONS	*Kvamme*
3:00– 3:45	COMMUNICATIONS CIRCUITS	*Hirshfeld*
3:45– 4:15	FUTURE TRENDS FOR LINEAR DEVICES	*Widlar*
4:15– 5:30	INTEGRATED CIRCUIT CLINIC	*Kalb, Thorkelson, Widlar, Hirshfeld & Kvamme*

If somebody's grabbed the coupon below, send $15 to Regis McKenna at National Semiconductor, 2975 San Ysidro Way, Santa Clara, California 95051.

National Semiconductor Corporation
2975 San Ysidro Way
Santa Clara, California 95051
Reserve me a spot *instantly* at *The* IC Seminar.
Here's my check for $15 to cover everything:

Name_____
Title_____
Company_____
Address_____
City_____State_____Zip_____

National Semiconductor

Bob Widlar and Chips, our dog, and I plotted tech's future at our Saratoga, CA home. National Semiconductor labeled us Guru (Bob) and Wizard (me) to promote its conference in Paris.

leased. The building had a small fabrication facility. There, Bob designed the industry's first voltage regulator, the National LM100. Again, this was a new first in the analog circuit world. Shortly after, Bob announced the first upgrade to his uA709 Fairchild design, the National LM101. Both products were on the market before National hired Charlie Sporck, who would go on to lead National to global prominence.

Somehow, Bob's alcoholism did not obstruct his productivity. He not only designed circuits. He also prepared the marketing materials for them. By that, I mean data sheets, application notes, and FAQs (Frequently Asked Questions). The FAQs were particularly valuable in marketing and promoting Bob's products. He kept careful track of every customer query, and he kept a file of answers. He responded to a letter by asking his assistant to go to the file with the numbered answers and then write a letter, following his template with standard opening and closing paragraphs.

Snail mail was all we had in 1967. Still, Bob responded to customer inquiries faster than anyone else I knew. He was the full package.

When Charlie Sporck and his team (which included me) came to National in February 1967, Bob's innovative, brilliantly designed products immediately gave us something to build on. And wisely, we let Bob be Bob. When National reduced the frequency of grass-cutting outside Bob's office, he devised his own creative solution. One day, he showed up with a sheep. He placed the sheep on the grass outside his office, tied the animal to a tether, and used the sheep to trim his lawn.

Bob left National to be an independent design consultant for a variety of other analog semiconductor producers, including Linear Technology. I was sorry to see him go. We kept in touch, and in fact, he asked me to be his arbitrator in a dispute with some companies he worked for. I gladly accepted the role.

Bob moved to Mexico, continued his alcoholic ways, and died of a heart attack at age 53: a sad ending to a brilliant life.

CHAPTER 32

Jack Tramiel

JACK TRAMIEL IS NOT talked about anymore in the Valley, but in 1970, he was a famous character for anyone doing business in low-end computers, calculators, and other consumer gadgets. His brand was Commodore. He started the company in 1956 by signing a deal with an Italian typewriter manufacturer and using typewriter parts to set up Commodore Business Machines in Toronto, Ontario, Canada. Jack, who was born in Poland and immigrated to America in 1947, was one tough businessman. He would show off his toughness by displaying the Nazi-placed marks on his forearm, identifying him as a Jew who had survived the Holocaust.

Jack was famous for a number of things, but the one that stood out to me was that he would inevitably end up suing his suppliers or getting sued by them for any one of a number of reasons as his contracts aged. Usually, the lawsuits were introduced by the suppliers who contended that Jack had not lived up to his commitment in a deal.

Jack became interested in a simple calculator product that National Semiconductor was introducing and indicated a willingness to place a large order for millions of units. The product was simple. Building a calculator required assembling a single semiconductor chip, an LED (Light Emitting Diode) display, a keypad, an ON/OFF switch, a simple circuit board, a case, and a battery clip.

The problem was that National was planning to introduce the same product in its newly formed Consumer Products group. Jack would have to depend on us to supply his needs, and we could not favor our internal customers if our supply got short. We saw this as a challenging situation, particularly given Jack's tendency to sue his suppliers for practically no reason.

I decided we should have a dinner meeting to sort matters out with Jack. We had six or eight people, and we put Jack and his team on one side of the table, and me and my team on the other side. Throughout dinner, we had a pleasant conversation about the shipping and pricing and other details of our agreement. As we were wrapping up over dessert, Jack said something along the lines of "we should get the lawyers involved to finalize the deal."

I responded, to the surprise of my team members, by asking, "Do you need a contract?"

Jack clearly was not expecting this response. "Don't you?" he replied.

I stuck out my hand and said, "I just want your assurance that if I ship you the parts, you will pay me."

"Agreed," he said. And the deal was done.

What, you ask, was my thinking? I knew that I was dealing with a notorious plaintiff. I agreed to ship him millions of dollars of parts with no contract precisely because Jack had shown little respect for other contracts he had signed. I realized: What was yet another contract to Jack? It wasn't worth the paper it's written on. Furthermore, Jack knew that I had the upper hand in that I could always distribute those products to my internal customers, even though they didn't have the market reach of Commodore at the time.

I later learned that Jack's agreements with his customers required him to get paid in advance (or with very low days receivable) so he collected the cash for some units before even receiving them. If his product took off—which it did—he had a money machine that would run for a while. And it did.

Here is what really mattered though. This low-end computer was bound to turn very competitive, and it did. We agreed to "share" the profits available, which required me to lower our pricing to Commodore and Jack to lower his selling price to the end user. Our relationship was solid even though challenging. I'm happy to tell you that Jack paid us every dime he owed us. The deal rewarded both of us, and Jack honored his word.

CHAPTER 33

Steve Jobs

I MET STEVE JOBS in the late summer of 1982. This was six years after Steve had co-founded Apple with Steve Wozniak and my friend, Mike Markkula, and two years since the company went public. Apple was growing rapidly and closing in on its first $1 billion revenue year. The Apple II, the company's pioneering home computer introduced in 1977, had become its biggest seller. The Apple III, a business-oriented personal computer released three years later, was not enjoying much market success. Apple's CEO at this time was Mike (A. C.) Markkula, who had been the key angel investor who enabled the two Steves—Jobs and Wozniak—to incorporate as a company and manufacture their inventions at scale.

Mike was a friend. In 1966, I had hired him into Fairchild Semiconductor, where he worked in our linear circuit product marketing department. Mike and I both left Fairchild within the next year or so. I went to National Semiconductor, while Mike joined Intel just as it was starting. When I met Steve in 1982, I was President of National Semiconductor's National Advanced Systems unit, where we manufactured and marketed mainframe computer systems to IT departments. Our primary competition was IBM and Amdahl.

Mike called to see if I would be interested in coming over to Apple to run Marketing and Sales. The position, Executive Vice President of Marketing and Sales, would have three principal direct reports: Marketing (which was really advertising), Sales, and Distribution. Two of the people running those functions were National Semiconductor alumni and well known to me: Gene Carter, who ran Sales, and Roy Weaver, who headed Distribution. Fred Hoar, whom I didn't know, was the Marketing executive. At the time, Steve Jobs was the Director of the MacIntosh unit and Chairman of the Apple board.

I told Mike that I was indeed interested in the EVP role. My first interview was about 15 minutes long. Mike and I walked into Steve's office area, and with all three of us standing there, we talked briefly. Steve was mildly friendly. I walked away unsure what he thought of me. I was self-conscious for two reasons: 1.) I came from the "boring" mainframe computer business and 2.) anyone over 40 years old, it was said at the time, doesn't know computers. I was approaching 45 years old at the time. Steve was 27. Being more than 15 years older than Steve was clearly not a plus.

After that first meeting with Steve came interviews with other members of Apple's board of directors, including Teledyne co-founder and CEO Henry Singleton, renowned tech investor Arthur Rock, Macy's executive Phil Schlein, and Peter Crisp of Venrock, the Rockefeller Family investment arm. For its relatively moderate size and stock market value, Apple had a most impressive board. I found these meetings to be quite challenging. Arthur Rock, whom I flew to Aspen, Colorado to see, probed me about my knowledge of consumer tech, which I really didn't have. I was used to selling mainframes to Chief Information Officers!

Despite my lack of relevant experience, I must have shown certain doggedness and eagerness to learn because I passed the directors' scrutiny. I got the job.

I was thrilled and excited to help Apple change the technology industry. Personal computing looked to me to be much more exciting than selling mainframe computers. I took some comfort in the fact that the PC and semiconductor industries shared a large variety of customer types, from consumers to large and small businesses to government and education buyers. The more forward-looking people who had been on my National Semiconductor staff, in fact, were already using these new PCs to improve their own productivity. Personal computing, I sensed, was poised to hit an inflection point of growth for both hobbyists and business professionals.

I must admit, I had never used a personal computer. That fact may be why my very first assignment was to go to a store and get one. I drove to the ComputerLand in nearby Mountain View and bought an Apple III. Back at my home office, I set it up myself. It wasn't easy.

Inside Apple, the Macintosh was a highly secretive project. No one gained access to the Macintosh development lab without careful screening by Steve. Meaning: Essentially, no one gained access. In that sense, Apple's culture was very closed and tight. But in another sense, the Apple culture was wonderfully open and forward-leaning. The attitude was "We can do anything." And we—that is, Steve and his team—really did believe that we were making insanely great products that would change the world.

CHAPTER 34

The Mac

AS I SETTLED IN and felt more comfortable at Apple, I was taken by Steve. I saw, up close, the perfectionism that he later became famous for. He worried, or at least fretted, about every detail of the Macintosh. The development of the Macintosh—or "the Mac," as we started to call it—had been going on for several years and was now reaching the end game: Apple was scheduled to introduce the Mac in June 1983. That was just eight months away. In the meantime, two other important development projects, the Lisa and the Apple IIe computers, were on the launch docket for January.

With multiple new products in the pipeline, the stress on our entire team was intense. The onus was on me, as the new EVP of Marketing and Sales, to deliver ever-increasing sales of existing products and stage a successful introduction of both the Lisa and the IIe—and then, this new computer called the Macintosh, which was coming along in Steve Jobs' back room.

The Lisa announcement went better than I or anyone else could have expected. The event could have been subtitled "The Mouse That Roared." Most of the press and the analysts had never seen a mouse-based point-and-click operating system, and the Lisa dazzled them. Steve had first seen a mouse during his 1979 visit to Xerox Park, recognized the device's transformative power for computing, and brought the mouse to Apple. Unfortunately, the Lisa ended up not performing well in the marketplace, largely because it was expensive and not compatible with other systems.

The new Apple IIe, meanwhile, was well received and taught us an important marketing lesson. During my drive home one night as I heard an ad for the IIe on the radio, I was struck that we were asking parents to buy a computer and teach their children to use it. I realized that the ad made no sense: Virtually no parents were qualified or felt qualified to teach their children how to use a computer. This was the dawn of the personal computer revolution, when it was the kids, not their parents, who were newly tech savvy.

As soon as I got home, I called the executive responsible for the ad. I told her that the ad was fundamentally wrong in its approach. She agreed. She got the ad changed to reflect the reality that kids were savvier about computers than their parents. Fortunately, changing audio in a radio ad in those days took only minutes. Sales of the new Apple IIe surged.

Apple's original plan, established before my arrival, was to introduce the Lisa and the Mac simultaneously, since both machines employ the innovative mouse. Early in 1983, however, Steve had decided that the hard-shelled floppy disk drive, code-named Twiggy, that was being developed for these two computer systems was not going to work on the Mac. Steve decided to use the more modern floppy disk on the Mac. As a result, the Lisa was introduced first, with its Twiggy disk, while the launch of the Mac was delayed until early 1984.

There was a humorous—in retrospect—incident on the way to finalizing the choice of the disk drive for the Mac. One day in early 1983, I got a call from an executive I knew at Hitachi, asking if I would introduce his people in Hitachi's hard-shelled floppy disk group to Steve Jobs. Steve agreed to a meeting, but not enthusiastically because he was already working with Sony, Hitachi's rival, on the hard-shelled floppy disk planned for the Mac and the Lisa. When the Hitachi people came to Apple's headquarters, which were then on Bandley Drive in Cupertino, they delivered a good presentation. Good, that is, until the Hitachi executive closed with one glaring error: He held up Hitachi's proposed three-inch disk for the Mac, and with a theatrical flourish, he slipped it into his shirt pocket.

The Hitachi man had clearly made his pitch with a belief that the Mac's disk needed to be small enough to fit easily into a shirt pocket. In contrast, our floppy disk, which Steve and his small team were developing with Sony, was three and a half inches wide. When the Hitachi executive tried to slip that disk into his shirt pocket, it didn't fit. At that moment, Steve picked up the Sony disk, larger than Hitachi's by one half inch, and slipped it deftly into his own shirt pocket.

We all learned lessons that day. We learned that Japanese shirt pockets are narrower than U.S.-made shirt pockets. Hitachi learned that American shirt pockets are more than three and a half inches wide. Obviously, this was a very embarrassing meeting for the Hitachi folks. It stunned me that they screwed up as they did. In any case, the Sony floppy disk dimensions, three and a half inches, went on to become the industry standard, primarily due to Apple's endorsement.

CHAPTER 35

Focus

IN 1983, THE PEOPLE working on the Apple II line of computers were a bit jealous of the attention paid to the Lisa and the upcoming Macintosh. People in the Apple II unit were grousing about the paucity of support they were getting. Wanting to address the unrest as well as set strategy for the future of the company, Steve Jobs gathered a dozen of his senior executives in a conference room.

"What's the most important thing for us to work on in the next year?" Steve asked us.

In a noisy free-for-all discussion, everyone in the room threw out answers. I was the guy doing the writing on the whiteboard. I recall listing about 40 ideas.

Then Steve asked: "What are the 10 most important things for us to work on in the next year?"

At that, everyone noted their favorites from the list on the whiteboard. That's how we voted.

Then Steve asked: "What is the No. 1 most important thing for us to work on in the next year?"

The winner: a successful intro of the Mac.

I'll never forget that constructive exercise and valuable lesson. We needed to get everyone on the same page—believing in what to focus on. To accomplish that, Steve gave everyone a vote.

I don't know what would have happened if the launch of the Macintosh had not won the contest. Clearly, the Mac was Steve's priority. And everyone in the room that day agreed with Steve because he was a leader who masterfully engendered followership.

In any case, the exercise solidified our commitment to focus on the Mac. The launch of the Macintosh was wildly successful—and the rest is history.

CHAPTER 36

1984

BEFORE THE REST of the world heard of the Mac, Steve Jobs met with Ridley Scott, the famous movie director. Apple's ad agency, Chiat/Day, had hired Scott, who had just had a megahit in Blade Runner, to direct commercials for the Lisa and the new Macintosh computer. The Lisa ad was called "Alone Again." It touted Lisa's advanced technology—

the pioneering mouse and a graphical interface—and portrayed Apple as leading the industry to a brighter future.

The Macintosh ad, meanwhile, cast Apple as the creator of a truly "personal" computer for everyone, free from the clutch of "Big Brother"—a thinly disguised IBM. The ad was called "1984," which was a reference to the Mac's upcoming launch year and to George Orwell's dystopian social science fiction novel that warned about the control and power of totalitarian regimes.

I first saw the storyboards for the Macintosh ads early in the summer of 1983. I am not a movie buff and wanted to have them evaluated since this campaign was going to be expensive. I had a friend who directed movies, so I took the boards to his home in the Santa Cruz mountains to get his opinion. My friend was blown away. In fact, he pleaded for an opportunity to make the commercials. That was not in my purview. Steve was making those arrangements. But I did walk away feeling that these would, in all likelihood, be special ads.

That October, at Apple's 1983 sales conference in Hawaii, we showed the "1984" commercial to the salesforce. Our salespeople went wild, whooping and pounding their fists on the tables. I concluded that we had a real winner.

Then came the bad news.

The Lisa, introduced that previous January, was not performing well in the marketplace. With sales flagging, Apple's board of directors was skeptical about plans to spend big to launch another new computer. The board deemed our plan to run ads across all the New Year's Day Bowl games too expensive. I was directed to cancel our ad commitment. I was loath to do that, particularly after that jubilant reception in Hawaii. Bill Campbell, who headed Apple marketing, was on the same page. We wanted to run the "1984" ad. We had promised it to the salesforce.

As December rolled along, we came up with the idea of making the

"1984" ad a Super Bowl commercial. In my mind, that idea carried an additional major risk. The ad would run on January 24. What if the "1984" theme was, by that time, used by other advertisers and "old hat"? I thought a late January run was very risky. But it was our only option to reach the massive audience we wanted. We decided to buy a 60-second block of airtime and two 30-second spots during Super Bowl XVIII. I can't recall the exact cost of the one-minute slot, but I know that each 30-second block cost $383,000.

On Friday before Super Bowl Sunday, Bill Campbell and I met in my office to review the situation before we confirmed our purchase with CBS. Suddenly, Jane Richardson, one of Apple's top ad executives, knocked on my door. "I have some news," she told us urgently. She explained that another advertiser was offering to pay Apple $700,000 to cede its Super Bowl minute. Bill and I looked at one another. One of us said, "Did she say something?!" That's how we ignored Jane's news. We instructed her to finalize our commitment to buy the time from CBS.

I don't remember ever being as insubordinate as I was that day.

The game, which had the Washington Redskins facing off against the Los Angeles Raiders, started at 4:30 p.m. We were not given a specific time when our ad would run. At least I don't recall one. The moment came during the third quarter, after a touchdown by the Raiders: As the ad opens, we see a room full of people with shaved heads, staring at and listening to a Big Brother character who is preaching the value of "unification of thought." A powerful blonde woman, dressed in orange shorts and a white tank top, runs into the room and heaves a sledgehammer at the screen—which explodes, revealing a message: "On January 24th Apple Computer will introduce Macintosh. And you'll see why 1984 won't be like '1984.'"

The commercial closes with Apple's rainbow logo—no image of the product or mention of its features.

The positive reaction was an immediate global groundswell. In the days that followed, TV stations everywhere were requesting the ad so they could run it during their newscasts. The ad became iconic. It won "Ad of the Year" in many polls, and ad of the decade and consideration for "ad of the century." Even though Apple ran the commercial only that one time.

I didn't ever tell anyone about the "offer" to buy our Super Bowl minute. No one at Apple ever asked. And no one ever questioned that big, risky expenditure.

By the way, I know of no other commercial that ran on the 1984 theme. We were "alone again."

Insubordination is okay if you are right.

CHAPTER 37

Idiot Proof

WHEN I WAS GROWING UP in San Francisco, the first family car that I can remember was a 1936 Chevrolet. How we managed to fit two adults and five children into that vehicle is a blur in my mind. I do recall that Dad was always the driver. This was the norm back then, when driving a car was not nearly as easy as it is today. Our Chevy had a stick shift and no power steering, nor many other features that are now commonplace.

Then, when I was 11 years old, Dad bought a 1949 Pontiac sedan with an automatic transmission. Now, Mom could drive. The investment in the new car gave her all sorts of new freedoms. She could now drive, rather than walk, to the grocery store. That one thing made my parents realize that it might make sense to move our family to a larger home in the suburbs.

Decades later, when I was at Apple, I thought about this example of a new technology—a car with an automatic transmission—changing lives in the most practical ways. Apple had just introduced mouse-based computing to the market. Our newest product was the Lisa, and its attention-grabbing feature was the mouse. The mouse dazzled analysts and fascinated consumers, who realized that they no longer needed to know computer programming language to enjoy the benefits of using a desktop computer.

Ease of use became our primary selling feature. Steve Jobs articulated the wonders of personal computing and the importance of ease of use when he described personal computers as "bicycles for the mind." In 1980, Steve said, "When we invented the personal computer, we created a new kind of bicycle... a new man-machine partnership." A two-page Apple ad in Scientific American further explained his quote, noting that while human beings are not as fast runners as many other species, a human on a bicycle can beat many of them. At Apple, from the earliest days on, we prioritized ease of use and committed to using increasing processing capability to make our machines easier to use, not just compute more.

Inside the labs, meanwhile, some developers thought their job was to make our computers "idiot-proof." That term was bandied about the entire computer industry, and I couldn't stand it. "Idiot-proof" demeans the computer user. It also misses the typical intent of new technology, which is to improve the way people live and work. Think about it: You don't have to be a pilot to travel in airplanes; you don't have to be a mechanic to drive an automobile; you don't have to know the principles of heat transfer to use a refrigerator. I could go on and on.

Here's how I see it: You will enjoy the full fruits of a technology business—or any business—only if you recognize that you are really in the service business. The ultimate user of your product deserves great respect and also deserves the "service" of making the product easy to set up and use.

And I would never call anyone who buys my ingenious product an "idiot."

CHAPTER 38

More Steve Stories

STEVE WAS A DEMANDING, exacting, and fascinating person to work with. In time, I came to enjoy him very much, though the feeling, I know, was not always mutual. Steve's perfectionism affected many other areas of his life. In the decade since Steve passed away, numerous books and articles have detailed various aspects of the history of both Steve and Apple. The deep storytelling is well deserved because both the man and the company he created are remarkable—and changed the ways people around the world live and work.

I've come to call these various vignettes "Steve Stories." I'll share a few Steve Stories that perhaps you haven't heard before.

One day in 1983, I was at Steve's home in Los Gatos, reviewing aspects of the upcoming Mac launch. It was just the two of us going over the plan in his pristine living room, which contained a piano and a sofa. Only a piano and a sofa. As I was leaving, Steve asked me if I would do him a favor. He told me that he was meeting a new "date" in a few hours, and he wanted me to listen to a piano piece that he had been working on and planned to play that evening. I don't recall if Steve had written the piece or had just learned to play it. In any case, Steve sat down at his piano and played the piece. It was beautiful and romantic.

When he asked for my reaction, I replied: "It's beautiful. If the girl doesn't like it, you should drop her immediately since, in my opinion, anyone not liking that piece is not someone to hang around with." He smiled, clearly pleased by my reaction.

In all the years that I knew Steve and in the decade since his passing, I've never heard or read anything about his musical ability. A few books about Apple's history note the extraordinary gift that Steve bought for the Macintosh development team in 1984: a Bösendorfer grand piano, which is one of the finest pianos in the world. The Bösendorfer sat in Apple's lobby, for the Mac developers to play on their breaks from their intense work.

Another story that will give you a sense of what a risk-embracing outlier Steve Jobs was: In 1985, Steve was pushed out of his own company by a CEO he had brought in, John Sculley, and Apple's board of directors. Shortly after this stunning turn of events, Steve made his first visit to Pixar, the computer animation company then known as Graphics Group and part of George Lucas's film company. Steve was preparing to invest $5 million as a first step in a plan to buy Graphics Group from Lucasfilm. (In 1986, Lucasfilm spun out Graphics Group, and Steve became its majority shareholder.)

Steve asked me to go along with him for his first visit to Pixar. I gladly accepted, and he picked me up in his new black Porsche. As we drove north from the Valley toward Pixar's offices, then in Marin County, our route took us through San Francisco's Golden Gate Park. Entering the park, we noticed a policeman, with his red lights lit, following us and motioning Steve to pull over. Steve pulled over.

"I wonder what the problem is," I said to Steve. "I don't think you were speeding."

"I know," Steve replied, seemingly confident that he knew exactly why the policeman stopped us. "I don't believe in license plates," Steve added. Then he pulled two license plates from the glove compartment of his Porsche. He rolled down his driver side window, showed the plates to the officer, and talked the cop out of issuing him a ticket. I sat in the passenger seat with my mouth open, in awe of the whole scene.

As we left the scene and drove on, I got an earful from Steve about the color of the California plates. The plates—white with blue numbers, and "California" in red capital letters on top and "The Golden State" in yellow regular type at the bottom—ruined the look of his Porsche, Steve said. That is why he did not want to install the license plates.

The look of a product, inside and out, always mattered to Steve. At the time of the Lisa introduction, Steve had never been in a "raised floor" data center room. A "raised floor" is an elevated floor, traditionally part of data centers, that creates a space that can be used for cooling, electrical, and mechanical services. Our team wanted to show the Lisa in this kind of data center because we wanted to promote the idea of our new machine as a smart terminal in an IBM environment.

I called John Cullinane, the CEO and co-founder of Cullinet Software, which competed with IBM in the database software world, and asked him to join our Lisa demo. John agreed. We arranged with the CIO of American President Lines, a container shipping company, to use his data center on the San Francisco Peninsula. As the cameras were moving into position, Steve and I were standing next to one of the IBM mainframes when I asked him if he wanted to see the inside of the machine. I opened the mainframe, exposing a sea of wires that made up the hardware connections. Steve was aghast.

"What is all this s—t?" he asked. He peered inside the box that looked as if some amateur had thrown it together. Seeing that "rat's nest," as he called it, inside the IBM mainframe diminished Steve's respect for IBM's overall product line. To him, such sloppy workmanship denigrated the value of the product and made it much less serviceable.

In a way, that day in the American President Lines data center caused Steve to worry less about the prospect of IBM introducing "insanely great products." In his mind, "insanely great" was impossible at IBM—and eminently doable at Apple.

My favorite "Steve the perfectionist" story occurred about two weeks ahead of Apple's January 1984 introduction of the Macintosh. I received a call from Roy Weaver, the Apple executive in charge of distribution of the product. Roy said that Steve had just come by to see him and rejected every one of the shipping boxes that we had received from the vendor. The reason Steve rejected them: The color of the cardboard was not the right white.

Mind you, we are talking about the packing box. Roy was upset—he had a tight budget and looming deadlines to meet to get this new computer, the Macintosh, into the market on schedule. Soon enough, Roy calmed down and told me the whole story, which made me realize that Apple had no choice but to make the packaging box cardboard the "right white." Roy made it happen. And sure enough, the Mac's white packaging box stood out boldly from the brown cardboard packaging of competitive products. Steve was right.

Someone once asked me how it was that Steve was so good at picking product features that made his products stand out. I'm sure there are many answers to that question, but among them, I would say that Steve's attention to what the vendors were doing was key.

Steve recognized that in those days, Apple hardware was an assemblage of vendor-supplied semiconductors, displays, memory products, and other parts. He spent a lot of time—and plenty of his own personal emotional energy—talking to the vendors and encouraging them to incorporate the features he wanted. Bigger established companies simply did not have a Steve Jobs inside their walls to take the time and make it so personal.

Also, Steve was not afraid to buy from a "sole source." In the computer industry at that time, it was common practice for chip users to insist on having a second source for all parts of a product; this way, purchasing departments could set two vendors up against one another and negotiate better pricing. Steve recognized that most of his competitors would, as standard practice, wait for a second source before moving a new computer model from development to production—and thus come to market later than a company relying on single source procurement. Using a sole source for each part of a new computer also enabled Apple to fulfill its mission to create "insanely great" products. They had the latest features.

When Steve tried to convince me not to leave Apple in 1984, he walked me through a secret project that he was working on in a Los Gatos hideaway: an "Apple phone." The board fired Steve soon after. Twelve years later, after Apple floundered with such ill-fated and overpriced devices as the Newton, the board wisely brought him back into the company. In 2007, with Steve back at the helm, Apple introduced the iPhone. He set a new standard in mobile communication and computing. Think about it: Not many Blackberries are being sold these days.

Like most other geniuses, Steve was not always easy to work with. Geniuses hate failure—they tolerate failure in themselves and other people less than the rest of us do. Working for Steve and knowing him over many years, I learned that the smartest way to behave with a genius—particularly a creative genius like he was—is to provide a long leash and a wide berth. At some point, you may need to say, "This isn't working." If you do, say it decisively but gently, and have your facts ready to back up your opinion.

CHAPTER 39

Amazon

IN THE MID TO LATE 1990s, investments in retail entities became quite popular. There were any number of WebVan type investments. Most of these companies failed to meet their projections, and some went under during or after the "correction" that occurred on Wall Street around 2000. One company that clearly did not fail was Amazon—although it was not a profitable company for a long time.

At Kleiner Perkins, John Doerr was introduced to Jeff Bezos by Bill Campbell, who was doing some consulting for our firm. John got involved with Amazon and, in fact, helped Jeff build his management team. After this period of initial interaction, John learned that Jeff was raising more funding for Amazon, and he invited Jeff to visit Kleiner Perkins to present to us. I remember Jeff came to the meeting alone. As I recall, it was going to be an expensive buy in that Amazon's pre-money valuation was in the $30 million range. That was the highest or near-highest valuation we had ever invested in.

In his presentation at our Palo Alto office, Bezos outlined his thinking on why books would be a great product to begin Amazon's growth journey. He was clear that he did not see Amazon as just a book dealer. He reasoned that people buying on his site were using a browser to find their items. That's what people do in a book shop—they browse. Starting with books made sense also, Jeff told us, because the availability of books from publishers was constant and straight-forward. Furthermore, books didn't suffer from loss by spoilage or other problems that grocers and many other retailers must contend with.

After the presentation, the partners met to review what we had heard.

We decided that we would go home that evening and buy books on the Amazon site so we could personally experience the purchase process. At the time, Jean and I were planning a trip to South America, which was to include a visit to the Galapagos Islands off the coast of Ecuador. I had begun the search for travel books about the Galapagos but hadn't found much yet. In fact, most bookstores I had visited did not offer a single book on the Galapagos Islands. That night, on Amazon.com, there were, I believe, six different titles. I had "choice."

The more I thought about that choice and ease of buying, the more the idea of buying books online appealed to me. I bought a copy of each of those Galapagos books that Amazon offered and received them in a reasonable time. At the follow-up partner meeting, I was affirmative on the investment, noting that the "choice" factor was major. Other partners found other reasons to like the deal, and we invested.

That isn't the end of the story. In its early years, Amazon was not a roaring success. It lost a lot of money as it grew. In later years, we learned to be patient investors since it took a while for the company to deliver on its promise of value. That is another lesson from the Amazon story. The company lost a lot of money but used available capital to build out its capability with its cash flow, while not having to pay taxes to the government. Amazon is a prime example of using cash wisely to build operational capability and, in the long term, one of the world's most successful and valuable companies.

CHAPTER 40

The Power of the Patent

SECTION 8 OF THE U.S. CONSTITUTION,
enumerating the duties of Congress, includes the following paragraph:

To promote the progress of Science and useful Arts, by securing for limited Times to Authors and Inventors the exclusive Right to their respective Writings and Discoveries;

Gaining a protective patent to keep the promise of an "exclusive Right" to certain technology is critical to many startups. A good example: the patent disputes that arose around patents issued to Power Integrations (POWI), a California-based supplier of integrated circuits. I sat on POWI's board for more than 30 years and witnessed the drama that can and did threaten the company's survival.

Power Integrations filed for and obtained a number of patents for a process by which high-voltage power, such as that supplied by the 110V/220V outlets common in our homes, can be converted to the low-voltage levels required by our phones, computers, entertainment systems, appliances, and any number of other gadgets that dominate our everyday lives. The somewhat unique feature of the patents that POWI secured is that engineers familiar with the technology claimed that the invention being protected was "obvious" to them. In other words, these knowledgeable engineers were saying, "Why didn't I think of that?" From the time of the company's founding, it was clear that POWI's hold on power conversion technology was going to rise or fall based on their patents.

The first infringement occurred in the 1990s, shortly after the founding of the company when a Motorola product was discovered to violate the patents. POWI sued. The court urged a settlement, but we knew we had a unique product in a growing market, and we were determined to protect that fully. If we made a royalty license arrangement, the courts would likely order us to make the same deal with other licensees.

As POWI's legal bills reached millions of dollars, direct CEO to CEO conversations provided no resolution. POWI won a lot of the legal battles in the seemingly endless war, but at tremendous cost. Virtually every verdict is contested by the losing party, adding to the legal costs. The lawyers are the only ones making any real money.

Had POWI not had strong patents, it could not have survived this onslaught. Today, POWI maintains its core of intellectual property exclusively and continues to serve its customers with competitive leading-edge solutions to power conversion requirements. As of this writing, all its lawsuits have been settled in POWI's favor, and the company remains the sole owner of the technology.

There is another story within this story that needs to be told. I am convinced that had this drama played out in the 1960s or 1970s when pretty much all the Valley executives knew one another—and respected each other even if they were the fiercest rivals in the market—such a patent fight would have been resolved quickly and settled amicably. The Valley of the 2000s was a far cry from the Valley of 1975.

CHAPTER 41

The Board of Directors

THE BOARD OF DIRECTORS of any company exists to oversee the operations of a company and represent the interests of shareholders. For better or worse, a corporate board plays an important role in determining the direction a company should take to meet its objectives. I've had the great pleasure to serve on more than 20 corporate boards. Some of those boards were very effective in helping the company reach its goals and its potential. Others were not.

Board members have a lot of power in a company, and there are principles that I've used to try to manage that power as effectively and responsibly as possible. In this chapter, I'll share some of those principles.

Let's start with this question: What is the board's responsibility?

I developed an answer to that question many years ago when I sat on the board of TriQuint Semiconductor with a gentleman named Ed Tuck. Ed told me that he came into each board meeting with two questions:

1. Should we fire the CEO?

2. If not, how can we help?

The longer I've served on boards, the more I like Ed's questions—and the more I've applied them to my own board experiences.

Regarding the first question, hiring and firing the CEO is the board's primary responsibility. If you've got the wrong leadership in the company, you are not going to perform properly. If you think the company has a wrong view of the market that it serves—or you believe that the chief marketing officer is the problem, you can discuss the problem with the CEO and share your point of view, but he or she is the ultimate decision-maker. If the board disagrees with the chief executive about strategy or personnel or some other issue, the board can advise, but it is the CEO who calls the shots. The board's option is to go along or fire the chief.

This tension between the board of directors and the CEO is natural, healthy, and inevitable. (If there is no tension at all, it's clear that neither the CEO nor the directors are pushing for growth and taking risks.) In some private (vs. publicly traded) companies, this board-CEO tension can get particularly sticky. For instance, if you have a board composed of investors who have not just financial stakes in the business but also interests in the company's technology for their own applications, you need to be sure that these investors never prioritize their personal interests.

And in some companies (public and private), methods of reporting financial data to the board can be problematic. Some companies prepare a "board package" to present financial results to the board that are in a different form than those used by management. I don't like this approach because the numbers are not the ones used by management to "run" the business. As a board member, I want to look at the data that are actually used by management. That way, I can be more helpful to management—and to shareholders.

The more grounded boards are in the reality of the company's day-to-day operations, the better off the company will be. When directors review certain operating units or divisions, the manager of that division should be in the boardroom. The manager typically understands the numbers and the nuances of the numbers better than a financial person. And given my marketing background, I like to hear about the positioning of a product or service via a brief presentation—yes, an elevator pitch. Keeping the marketing messages crisp always pays off.

If the board-CEO relationship is functioning properly and you don't need to fire the CEO (let's hope that's the case!), the second question is, "How can I help?" The answer relates to the reason you were chosen to sit on the board in the first place. Ask yourself: What do I bring to this company? You might have expertise in the company's industry, or perhaps you have deep experience in the international markets that the company intends to serve. Maybe the company's products involve new technology or sales channels that you understand well. There's a myriad of ways that directors can add value. A caution: The lifespan of expertise is short, especially in the tech industry. One day after you leave a company, you are one day out of date; one year after you leave, your knowledge may be irrelevant. Technology moves fast.

If you have expertise you hope to contribute to a company from a board perspective, do your best to keep current. It isn't easy, but it is necessary.

CHAPTER 42

Patience

IN THE MID 1980s, I was approached to look at a business plan that involved building integrated circuits with Gallium Arsenide (GaAs), a compound built from the elements gallium and arsenic. The plan suggested that GaAs technology could outperform silicon in a number of ways, and it would become a necessity as performance of electronic parts continued to improve. I had some familiarity with GaAs materials, having worked with them all the way back in 1961 when I was at General Electric's semiconductor division.

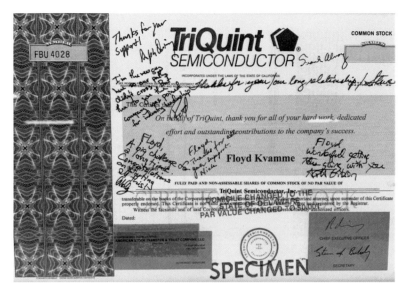

My gift from TriQuint when I retired from the board was a stock certificate with heartfelt notes penned by my fellow directors.

In the plan under review, there were compelling arguments in favor of launching the new venture, which was to be called Gazelle Microcircuits. The name was meant to convey the speed promised by the technology. As part of our diligence in evaluating the plan, we talked to the group at Tektronix in Oregon that was providing fabrication services to companies working with GaAs. Tektronix would do all of Gazelle's manufacturing with a model similar to that in the silicon world. Gazelle would make some "standard" products but was also marketing its capability to provide "custom" services for companies that had specific requirements.

After five years, sales were not good enough to meet the targets in the plan. There were promising areas of growth, but not enough for investors to continue funding the company. The board of Gazelle decided to explore merger opportunities. This led to the 1991 formation of TriQuint Semiconductor—a name that reflected the use of GaAs material, chemically known as a "3-5 material." Gigabit Logic, a California-based GaAs company, and the TriQuint division of Tektronix were also part of the merger.

Steve Sharp, a friend and fellow board member at Gazelle, and I agreed to form a search committee to find a CEO. The search turned out to be more difficult than we thought because none of the CEOs of the merging companies were interested in the job. We looked outside, without success. Finally, at one of our meetings, I turned to Steve and said, "I know who we should recommend. You."

Steve agreed and became the first CEO of TriQuint Semiconductor. He was an excellent choice. Steve saw the vision of the value of GaAs but also recognized that it was a splintered market, with many suppliers each having a small niche. There were a lot of ups and downs, but the long-term trajectory continued up and to the right. Steve stayed on for about 10 years and then yielded the CEO position to two other gentlemen over the subsequent 20 years.

Using GaAs and other materials to improve the performance of communications in today's near-wireless world has been the company's goal for many years. Success has required careful planning and minor and not so minor acquisitions. A merger with RF Micro Devices in 2014 was the big transition that catapulted the company.

Through it all, the lesson has been PATIENCE. And a realization that in the venture investing world, there are many examples of VCs investing too soon for the dream to materialize. But when you stick with it and build the puzzle piece by piece, you get rewarded with market power and great shareholder value.

A
New World
of Politics

The boss and me. In 2001, when George W. Bush became President,
I accepted an invitation to be one of his top technology advisors.

CHAPTER 43

My Entry Into The Political World

I'M OFTEN ASKED, "How did you get so involved with politics?" Here's the backstory.

I have always taken the responsibility to vote seriously. My parents voted in every election. A working-class family with five children was not generally able to put politics in their budget. So I doubt they ever contributed to a candidate. But they considered voting a civic duty, and they followed campaigns and candidates with great interest.

My dad was a "union Democrat" and used to comment on how the union made sure that the carpenters supported the issues and the candidates who fought for their best interests. Franklin Roosevelt was President when my folks could first vote, and I know they supported him. My dad liked Harry Truman (even though he expected Truman to lose to Dewey). I don't know if my parents, who voted for Democrats, actually switched their party affiliations in 1952, but I know they favored General Eisenhower. Having grown up in families that had been directly impacted by the war in Europe, both my parents respected Eisenhower's role in liberating Europe—and, by extension, their own families.

In 1956, my first presidential vote was cast for Eisenhower. I had registered as a Republican, but I was not active in the party. I don't remember ever going to a party event, although there were some taking place in Berkeley. With the "free speech movement" in full swing during my last years of school at Berkeley, my allegiance leaned Republican primarily because I found many promoters of the Democratic party to be not very likable people. They seemed crude in their approach to issues, and I was too busy studying to understand their beef with the existing system.

As I moved into my career in the semiconductor industry and my life as a husband and father of three boys, my schedule left little time for political involvement. Jean and I hosted a fundraiser for Ed Zschau when he ran for Senate in 1983, and we attended an event or two for folks running for Congress. But we went to no "party" functions.

That all changed in the early 1990s, when I was at Kleiner Perkins. I was interfacing with Montgomery Securities regularly. They were interested in being the banker for Silicon Valley companies that were looking to go public or needed bank services. At that time, Thom Weisel was running the venture activity at Montgomery Securities. Thom approached me about supporting a group called Empower America, where he served as Chairman.

Empower America had been founded by four Republican luminaries who were center-right in their philosophy: Jack Kemp, William Bennett, Jeane Kirkpatrick, and Vin Weber. Vin was a Congressman from Minnesota. Steve Forbes and Michael Novak were also deeply involved. These were impressive people who were well acquainted with the leadership of the Republican party.

I accepted Thom's invitation to attend a dinner at his home with my wife, Jean. Thom and his wife made a very good impression on us, and I was hooked. I paid the "entry" fee, $100,000 to join Empower America, and we attended their summer retreats in various Rocky Mountain resorts where members of Congress and the administration talked policy in gorgeous, intimate settings. It was interesting to hear how things really ran in Washington, D.C.

After a couple of years, Thom needed to step down as Chairman. He was busy running his new firm, Thomas Weisel Partners. Next thing I knew, I was accepting the Chairman's role. A board vote to approve me as chairman coincided with my holiday in Europe. I "attended" the board meeting by public pay phone in the middle of Normandy.

CHAPTER 44

All In

MY LEVEL OF POLITICAL engagement shot up via a phone call in August 1996. I was in a meeting in my office at Kleiner Perkins when my assistant came in and said that my wife was on the phone and needed to talk to me. This was highly unusual. Jean never called me at work unless there was an emergency or something urgent. The last such call I had gotten from Jean was 12 years earlier when she phoned to tell me that my father had passed away.

My concern was obvious, and in handing the call over to me, my assistant assured me by kindly saying, "No one died." I picked up the phone and immediately heard: "They are doing it again!" I logically asked Jean who are "they", and what are they "doing"?

As she calmed down, she explained that the San Jose newspaper, The Mercury News, was reporting that Silicon Valley executives were supporting Bill Clinton over Bob Dole by a huge margin. We knew that this was not true. And couldn't let it come true because we knew and liked Jack Kemp, Dole's running mate on the Republican ticket.

Jean's solution was a "marching order" to me: "You have got to do something!" she said.

I got the point and the urgency of the situation. I was now in POLITICS. And I had a valuable base. My longtime presence in Silicon Valley plus my activities with Empower America gave me a Rolodex, so to speak. Within no time, our living room was converted into a mail center. Fortunately, Jean had a home-based business, Service Partners Limited, which supported the meeting planning industry. Jean's company arranged meetings for corporate clients and had expertise in managing mail lists. This capability was a huge asset. We didn't have to bring in pricey outside services to reach potential supporters.

Unaware of rules and regulations around political engagement, I did what seemed to me to be a natural first step: I wrote a letter to a dozen or so CEOs, asking them if we could include their signatures in an ad in The Mercury News. We were seeking five times as many signatures as the Democrats had just displayed in their Mercury News ad. Jean's makeshift mailroom got the letter out, and the response was very positive. We collected the signatures—even more than we had targeted—and created the ad. The ad drew plenty of press attention to the realities of Silicon Valley politics: Republican support was alive and strong.

Amidst all this activity, I was encouraged to see a campaign consultant named Fred Lowell to make sure I was following all the rules and regs of political campaigns. As I described what I had done to Fred, who was a lawyer, he kept interjecting: "You did what?!" As I went on, Fred's level of disbelief escalated.

Since I had personally funded virtually all of the work, I had broken virtually every campaign finance law. Who knew?! I certainly didn't. Until Fred told me. He bailed me out by making me an "independent expenditure committee." This setup passed legal muster because I had not coordinated with the official campaign at all throughout my activities in support of Bob Dole for President.

If you are inclined to get involved with politics—and I hope you are— my advice is this: Know the reporting rules first. This will ease some later stress and strain.

CHAPTER 45

Silicon Valley Politics

THE 1996 ELECTION was a milestone in Silicon Valley. For the first time in my recollection, Valley leaders on both sides of the political divide had come together to support two ballot propositions. One increased the number of charter schools that could operate in the state; the other modified the procedure whereby companies could be sued in class action suits. The charter school initiative had good support across California, and with the huge investment of the tech community, it won by a large margin.

While I had also actively supported the Dole/Kemp presidential ticket, John Doerr, my partner at Kleiner Perkins, had been active in the campaign to reelect Bill Clinton.

John came to my office shortly after the election and suggested that it might be time for the technology industry to form its own association. His reasoning was that the American Electronics Association was too large and not adequately representing the critical issues of Silicon Valley-based companies. While semiconductor manufacturers were benefiting from the work of the Semiconductor Industry Association, they would welcome another association to represent the non-semiconductor parts of the technology industry. A healthy tech industry, after all, would benefit the chip makers.

John asked if I thought the Republicans whom I had brought together in the recent election would join such an organization representing Silicon Valley interests. He had already talked to Democrats who had worked with him and found them open to the idea. I told John that I would gauge the interest of the GOP crowd. I polled a group of more than 50 Valley Republicans and found a willingness on the R side.

The Technology Network, or TechNet as we preferred to call it, was born in 1997. It was structured to be a national bipartisan network of technology CEOs and senior executives. It had a Democrat and a Republican side. When a political candidate came to the Valley, either the D or the R side would arrange to sponsor a gathering. The result? A lot of candidates visited the Valley with the goal of getting financial support.

I accepted an invitation to take the lead Republican role at the organization. I worked with Lezlee Westine, who ran the group's Republican branch. Lezlee had serious political chops, having worked for California Governor Pete Wilson for several years before joining TechNet.

Governor George W. Bush was visiting the Valley, and I, as the Republican lead at TechNet, was the person designated to greet and brief him about the issues that most concerned our members. This was the summer of 1998, and there was already a lot of buzz about who the Republicans would nominate to run against Al Gore, the presumptive Democratic nominee. All bets were on George W. Bush.

The governor was quite accommodating as we discussed the issues, but seemed to shy away from any questions that related to his potentially running for the presidency. As we sat side by side at a luncheon table, I told him that most people in the room came because of those rumors that he was going to run for president.

Kvamme wields influence in Silicon Valley, Washington

VENTURE CAPITALIST TO LEAD BUSH TECH-ADVISORY PANEL

By Matt Marshall
Mercury News

Twelve years ago, venture capitalist Floyd Kvamme feared that a company he invested in, Gazelle Microelectronics, was on the brink of failure.

Kvamme flew to Washington. He convinced executives at a government defense research agency that the company's business — making chips from a new material to facilitate optical networking — was a key technology.

Kvamme came back with a $5 million grant. It saved the company, which at one point came within three days of bankruptcy. "He was an evangelist for the company," says Steven Sharp, a board member who has since become

chief executive of Gazelle's successor, Triquint Semiconductor.

On March 28, President Bush named Kvamme, 62, co-chair of the President's Committee of Advisors on Science and Technology. Kvamme will play a key coordinating role on technology policy issues and serve as White House emissary to Silicon Valley.

He was chosen for his potent skills of diplomacy, of the kind he showed at Gazelle.

"I can think of no better coordinator than Floyd," Bush said. "He is an entrepreneur, he is a risk-taker, he understands risk and reward. . . . He knows

See **KVAMME**, *Page 4C*

Floyd Kvamme saddles Alejandro, a Peruvian Paso, for a morning ride in the Santa Cruz Mountains in 1998.

RICK E. MARTIN
MERCURY NEWS
ARCHIVES

THOR SWIFT

Gov. Pete Wilson, *at podium, addresses students at a charter public schools bill-signing ceremony held at San Carlos Learning Center last May, as TechNet President Reed Hastings, center, and TechNet executive committee member Floyd Kvamme look on.*

By Bobby McGill
SPECIAL TO THE EXAMINER

SCARCELY A YEAR OLD, the Technology Network, a Palo Alto-based consortium of high-tech industry leaders, is fast becoming a major presence in shaping Washington's perception of Silicon Valley.

With well-funded, nar-

Silicon Valley starts feeling

"When we first started this, it was clear that most politicians saw Silicon Valley as nothing but a fund-raising base," said Schnur. "The overriding sentiment in the valley has always been very libertarian: 'We'll leave the politicians alone if they leave us alone.'"

That has certainly changed. Just this past week CRP released figures showing that large amounts of mon-

My new role in Washington brought countless opportunities to promote U.S. tech leadership. On my left are CA Gov. Pete Wilson and Reed Hastings, who headed the California State Board of Education soon after he founded Netflix.

Top: Kleiner Perkins' John Doerr is behind me on the left;
Reed Hastings is on the right end. Bottom: Congressman Ernie Konnyu,
me, Jean, and our sons Todd and Damon.

"I don't know what to do about that," the governor replied. "I do know that running for the presidency is tough on families."

Having twin 16-year-old daughters gave him pause, he explained. He gave me a rather long and, I must say, compelling explanation about how his concerns for his daughters' safety and well-being impacted his decision-making about his own future.

My takeaway was that he was not going to run. In fact, as he spoke on stage that day, a waiter dropped a load of dishes, and the tremendous bang sounded like a gun going off. I saw Governor Bush duck down behind the lectern. He knew how to duck and cover—and I thought to myself: He is not going to run. It's too dangerous.

In fact, I bet John Chambers, then the CEO of Cisco, and one other person on that. I lost both those bets.

CHAPTER 46

Signing on to the Bush Team

OUR NEXT MEETING came several months later when I was invited to one of the luncheons that Bush was hosting at the governor's mansion in Austin. He invited 40 or so people to join him for a discussion of the issues of concern to Texans and the business world. I was given the seat right next to the governor, which surprised me. He was very open and engaging. He had a deep interest in America's startup economy and the contributions it was making to domestic economic and job growth. Only later did I learn of Bush's attraction to the word "entrepreneur."

After the Austin visit, I was pretty much hooked. I had been to a small meeting with John McCain and felt that he was solely a foreign policy-oriented candidate. I sensed that his lack of interest in domestic policy would be a major problem in a general election. Meanwhile, I had confirmed that Jack Kemp, whom I had come to know well and liked very much, was not going to run. So, Bush was my man.

Bush came back to the Valley shortly after he announced his candidacy in June 1999. I agreed to head up a fundraiser. We convened 600 people at a luncheon at the Cabana Hotel in Palo Alto. That evening, John Chambers hosted an event at his home that raised $4 million for the Bush campaign.

I also accompanied George Bush on the campaign trail. I found a way to be useful: As questions concerning technology came up, the governor and his team would ask me for advice. One of our more interesting trips was with a group of Silicon Valley folks to New Hampshire prior to the primary. Lezlee Westine came along, as did a journalist with The Mercury News. After our first day of visits, which included college campuses and local companies, we met with campaign managers, who briefed us on the local issues.

That next morning, we ran into the candidate's mother, Barbara Bush, who was in town for a speaking engagement. She got a kick out of the shirts we all wore: "Reason for freezin' – George Bush." She asked how we were laundering them between daily usages. We told her the truth: We weren't. She laughed.

The weather was horrible on that trip. We were fighting a huge snowstorm. After a couple of meetings and rallies in the Concord/Manchester area, we headed up Highway 89 to Dartmouth. It was snowing heavily, and our driver was doing all he could to make sure we stayed on the road. Then, the windshield wipers gave way. I was assigned the duty of clearing the windshield. As I stuck my arm out the window to clear my side of the glass (and we repeatedly had to pull over to clear the windshield on the driver's side), we couldn't believe what we had gotten ourselves into. To us Californians, this winter wonderland adventure was almost comical.

After a terrible and at times terrifying ride, we arrived at Dartmouth. To say the reception was cool would be an understatement. It was no surprise to any of us who were on that trip when Governor Bush lost New Hampshire. And when Lezlee Westine asked Karl Rove if he would like our group to go anywhere else to help the campaign, he passed on the offer. I wasn't surprised.

All in all, the Valley served Candidate Bush well. When he came to the Valley a couple days before Election Day, I located an ideal place for a rally: a community help location. I knew the head of the San Jose Rescue Mission, and the optics were ideal to convey that Bush (who had his own skeletons, including a DUI years earlier) was a relatable guy and a man of the people. As he talked with some of the residents, he became so involved in their personal stories that he was late for his own speech.

As the event ended, I introduced Scott McNealy, the founder and CEO of Sun Microsystems, to Governor Bush. Scott had just returned from a road trip and told him that he was very concerned about the health and the direction of the U.S. economy. As the economy continued to slip during the early days of the Bush presidency, I often thought back on Scott's observation at that early point of economic slowdown.

Soon after Bush beat Al Gore in the 2000 election, I got a call from one of the Bush staffers, asking me if I had an interest in becoming a U.S. ambassador. Yes, I was at least a bit interested, I thought to myself. And if I could choose where to serve, I'd pick Japan. But Jean, my wife, made it clear that she did not want to move to Japan—or anywhere outside California.

"Ask for an Ambassador to Silicon Valley!" she told me.

Well, in some respects, that is what I did.

CHAPTER 47

Advising the President

Members of PCAST (President's Council of Advisors on Science and Technology) convene with President Bush.

I DID NOT TAKE ADVANTAGE of the opportunity to be an ambassador in the Bush White House. But in March 2001, I accepted an invitation to become Co-Chair of the President's Council of Advisors on Science and Technology, I considered it a new level of opportunity.

PCAST, as the Council is known, is an advisory group of America's leading scientists and engineers who directly advise the President. Franklin D. Roosevelt established the first presidential Science Advisory board in 1933. This board was an early iteration of PCAST. Ever since, PCAST has provided essential scientific and technical advice to the President of the United States. Moreover, it makes policy recommendations in areas where understanding of science, technology, and innovation is key to strengthening the economy and fulfilling the needs of the American people.

Serving in this important advisory role was fascinating and gratifying. To my amazement, I found that many of the "rules" that had governed my perception of being an effective advisor held true in the White House role. Such as: If you are an advisor, the most critical question to ask is, "In what areas does the advisee want the advisor to advise?" Advice that is not sought or not of interest to the one being advised is of little value!

Advice must be timely. If the advisee needs to make a decision in a few days, doing research that is sure to take months is simply a waste of time. This might seem obvious, but the world is full of armchair "advisors" who don't grasp the importance of timely decision-making—and even worse, advisors who critique decisions via "Monday morning quarterbacking." An executive doesn't need these types of advisors.

Advice must be not only accurate but also uninfluenced by any perceived bias of the advisee. Telling a person what they want to hear is of little value. Also, as an advisor, if you gain certain insight from someone in the process of forming your own point of view and your advice, you need to consider and, if necessary, openly acknowledge the biases and/or the agenda of this person.

As an advisor, you must watch vigilantly for situations that might result in a surprise to the person you're advising. Keep an eye out for issues that could blindside the client.

Here's how it worked inside the White House—where the rules for successful advising, I discovered, apply to most other advisory assignments. After I was appointed Co-Chair of PCAST in March 2001, I met with

White House staff to learn about the areas where they wanted us to focus our initial work. Neither the other Council members nor the White House Science Advisor had yet been named, so I was alone in representing PCAST in this initial meeting. President Bush's staff directed me to meet with various Cabinet Secretaries to gain their insights about the new administration's priorities around science and technology.

Meeting with the Secretaries was a wonderful opportunity to learn what was needed and what we could do. This was the first presidential administration where every Cabinet Secretary had an assigned tech advisor. Michael Dell, the founder of Texas-based Dell Computer, had convinced President Bush that new technologies were impacting the economy in critical ways. The existence of these designated tech advisors indicated that President Bush listened to Michael.

Clearly, President Bush was committed to learning how best to apply science, technology, and innovation to keep America strong. I learned early on that one of President Bush's favorite words is "entrepreneur." He talked a lot about entrepreneurs and always wanted to know what they were doing and how they were thinking.

I also learned that energy was a priority for President Bush. This was certainly no surprise given that the new President was a Texas man. Moreover, America was confronting a full-blown energy crisis. In 2000 and 2001, California was reeling from energy price spikes, rolling blackouts, and bankruptcies of major companies that literally kept the lights on across the state. The need for big fixes to America's energy infrastructure was urgent.

My first assignment, in May 2001, was to set up a meeting of members of the tech community, President Bush, California Governor Gray Davis, and Los Angeles Mayor Richard Riordan. The attacks on September 11 interrupted some of the plans for this important gathering. Moreover, John Marburger, my PCAST co-chair and the President's newly named science advisor, was not confirmed by the Senate until November, so our Council's first meeting with President Bush was delayed until December.

We spent the interim months constructing a list of 19 different areas that were of interest to the various Cabinet departments. This was a robust list, in part because of the Bush Administration's clear-eyed focus on technology.

The PCAST advisory board, meanwhile, was an impressive group of distinguished experts on science and technology. Some members had served on previous PCASTs. They were particularly helpful, clueing us in on the priorities and biases of many people who were suggesting policy ideas to us and otherwise offering to help.

At our first meeting with President Bush that December, he emphatically requested that we make our reports concise. He also asked us to include suggestions and opinions regarding first steps that the administration could take to address certain issues. Policy decisions resulting from this input, of course, rested with the administration.

Keep in mind: As an advisor at any level, you shouldn't expect that your advice will either be "rubber stamp" followed or that the decisions made will even be compatible with the policy that you suggested. Deciding is not the advisor's role; decisions based on the advice rest with the advisee.

In January 2005, during the inauguration festivities for President Bush's second term, my wife and I sat at a luncheon table with Vice President Dick Cheney. During our lunch, one gentleman at our table suggested to Mr. Cheney that new energy technologies such as wind and solar power were a tiny part of the energy picture and would remain so for decades to come. Sitting and listening to this, I had a hard time containing myself. Fully aware of the increasing interest in the energy sector that was sweeping through both the venture capital and private equity sectors, I totally disagreed with this man. But I felt I shouldn't interrupt.

After the luncheon, I sought out one of the event organizers to ask who that gentleman was. It was Lee Raymond, then CEO of ExxonMobil. I felt that I had to "correct" Raymond's input. The first opportunity came a couple of months later when I saw President Bush at an event in Los Angeles. In the snippet of time available, I told the president that entrepreneurs were attacking the energy field and making progress. "Entrepreneur", as mentioned earlier, was one of President Bush's favorite words. He responded with great interest and said that he wanted to hear about these developments.

President Bush's directive led to the drafting of a comprehensive report on more than 100 energy projects—representing areas such as biofuels, electricity generation, and energy efficiency—that were being supported by venture and private equity investors. The team I worked with on this report, a hardworking group of about a dozen people, completed the report in late 2005, though it was not released publicly until November 2006. It took a full year to wind its way through the federal government's approval maze and make it to the printing press!

Briefing the President in the Oval Office is an exciting experience, particularly when he brings in a dozen of his top officials—including, in this case, the Vice President and the Secretaries of Energy and Agriculture. With such an audience in the room, it's clear that the President values the advice he's getting. The entire experience of working with the Bush Administration was tremendously rewarding. Our report contributed to the president's robust support for new energy initiatives, which he announced in his 2006 State of the Union speech. These new initiatives fueled long-term efforts to reduce America's need for imported oil to zero. I'll talk more about this report in Chapter 51.

The results of the efforts are clear and impressive: Oil imports peaked in 2005 at 12.5 million barrels per day and fell to 11.3 million barrels per day in 2008—a 10% reduction in a three-year period, with biofuels and fracking increasing domestic supply. Today, net petroleum imports have been reduced to zero as a result of the policies recommended in our report as well as continuing productivity improvements by domestic oil companies.

Advising, particularly at the Presidential level, is hard work that requires the most diligent preparation. Seeing the advice result in policies that meet national goals is a very satisfying thing that makes every bit of effort worthwhile.

CHAPTER 48

The Perks of Politics

EVERYBODY TALKS ABOUT the downsides of working in politics. There are upsides too. While my work as Chairman of an Advisory Board to the President earned me no compensation and left me fewer hours in the day to do my main job, a few things made the political work special and truly worthwhile.

One was the thrill of certain surprise occasions. On one of President Bush's visits to California, he was making a stop in Sacramento on his way to the southern part of the state. I got a call inviting Jean and me to join the President on Air Force One for that leg of his visit. Jean had a schedule conflict and couldn't join me, but I was able to go.

Flying on Air Force One with the President of the United States is a once in a lifetime opportunity. I'll never forget the view after we took off in Sacramento: a flotilla of escort aircraft flew beside us. Once we hit cruising altitude, we—and four other special guests—were invited to join the President in his onboard office. What a thrill! President Bush

*Meeting with President Bush in his office on Air Force One
as we flew from Sacramento to Palm Springs*

steered the conversation to our interests. He and his staff made us feel very welcome and comfortable. I shall not forget that hour in Air Force One, as long as I live.

A ride in the President's limo followed. We watched the long black car being unloaded from a C-130 aircraft that had flown to southern California alongside us. Again, a unique experience watching the logistics of Presidential travel.

I sat in a seat behind the driver and right next to the President. That vehicle was amazing. The car door was by far the thickest and heaviest car door I had ever seen. I don't know what it weighed, but it was certainly in the multiple hundred-pound category. For 40 minutes or so as we rode to the venue where President Bush was due to speak, I got the chance to view a presidential parade from the inside—from the

President's vantage point. Another perk to treasure for a lifetime.

Another perk was the opportunity to attend the White House Christmas Party. What a festive event. If memory serves me, there are six or seven such parties each year. Over the years that I served President Bush, Jean and I attended six Christmas parties at the White House. Every one of these parties was a fabulous experience. The White House is decorated beautifully, and you get to mix with a couple hundred fellow supporters and members of the administration in a wide-open White House. The President and First Lady pose for a picture with each and every guest. Mr. and Mrs. Bush were always warm and engaging.

These are just three memories I'll carry with me forever. There are many other benefits of engaging in politics. I think being in Washington is one of them. I reject the notion that Washington, D.C. is a "swamp." Sure, you have to deal with policy positions pushed by the opposing party, but this is our nation's capital, and this is how America was set up to work; the push-pull of opposing groups and the need to find common ground. Moreover, Washington is the home of monuments that represent what America is and what we as Americans stand for. Walking from federal building to federal building gives you a sense of U.S. history that's impossible to match by reading books or seeing videos about the capital.

Those of us who live on the West coast don't have an opportunity to experience Washington frequently enough. That is unfortunate. America is still, to many people, the envy of the world. Our capital tells our story and should be heralded. We are not perfect, but we have a good story that needs to be told to each generation. Serving in Washington is a good way to keep our story alive.

CHAPTER 49

Brevity is Best

PARING YOUR TO-DO LIST to the most essential tasks helps you prioritize your workload and get the most important things done. The art of focus, broadly applied, typically pays off for everyone around you. In business, I've found, brevity typically is best. For instance, if you prepare a monthly report and it is typically five pages long, try cutting it to one page. When I was at Apple, my monthly report to our CEO was required to "tell all" and fit on one side of one piece of paper. It wasn't easy to summarize, but the one-page limitation worked to make the reports crisp and readable. The size limit assured that John Scully, then Apple's CEO, would actually read them.

Imagine if everything you write could be read in three to five minutes!

On another occasion while I was at National Semiconductor, I was scheduled to testify before a Congressional Committee in Washington. I was given 10 minutes for my formal remarks. I worked with my staff to prepare a concise 10-minute testimony—only to hear that my time had been reduced to five minutes! Then, at a meeting the night before my testimony, the time was cut again—to two minutes. I stayed up most of the night working on a concise version of my presentation. The result? My two-minute testimony was the most difficult one I ever had to prepare, but I discovered that it was possible to make all the key points that we had included in the 10-minute version.

I had another opportunity to test this brevity concept in Washington. We had prepared a major report on Energy. I was given 10 minutes to present to President Bush in the Oval Office. I worked hard on the presentation, as you might imagine—and felt the pressure on me particularly when I was told that the Vice President, the Secretaries of Energy and Agriculture, and a dozen other administration officials would be in the room. This time, the challenge would be that the President could, at any point in my presentation, interrupt to ask a question or make a comment. I was briefed on the importance of responding precisely and quickly getting back on point.

From these experiences in Washington, as well as others that required me to be both compelling and concise, I realized that most presentations are wordier than they need to be. Brevity requires work. What if all the 30-minute presentations you've sat through were cut to 10 minutes? Or five minutes? Yes, the presenter would have a tougher job paring it to the essential points, but the audience, I bet, would be rewarded—and more attentive.

CHAPTER 50

Computer Power

THROUGHOUT MY LONG CAREER in Silicon Valley, one issue, besides the threat of Japanese competitors, dominated the minds of the people who were building and leading companies: Power. By power, I mean the availability of energy to make the plants run. Semiconductor manufacturing requires two important commodities: water and electricity.

In the early 1970s, the issue of electricity availability started to rear its head. In those days, most Valley-based semiconductor companies did most of their wafer fabrication locally. Electricity was critical to the process. On one occasion, I recall discussions about rationing electricity—turning the power off for certain hours each day so users could get equal amounts of electricity "ON" time. Making wafers required a constant supply of electricity, and lengthy shutoffs would put the semiconductor companies out of business. So this threat sent some semiconductor manufacturers packing. They started moving manufacturing activities out of California to other states.

I was General Manager of the National Semiconductor operation during this period. We were determined to move wafer manufacturing out of the Valley to Texas, Maine, and Scotland. To make sure that the politicians comprehended the impact of electricity disruption on manufacturing, the industry visited Sacramento. Politicians got the message—but wafer fabrication and its high job count continued to stall in Silicon Valley. In the early 1970s, National stopped building new plants in the Valley. Across the industry, I know of no new plants built after the early 1980s.

These local power issues brought politicians to the Valley and opened doors for the leaders of semiconductor companies to meet with Senators and members of the House who represented other states now producing semiconductor products.

The governor of California during this period—specifically from 1975 to 1983—was Jerry Brown. He had hopes of becoming President some day and was very attentive to economic issues such as the impact of electricity reliability on some of his state's most important companies. Governor Brown had a friend, Regis McKenna, who was the best thing that ever happened to the Democrat party. Regis was positively eager and ever tireless in introducing Democratic politicians from across the country to Valley executives. Regis never seemed to care whether you were a Democrat or a Republican. Whatever your political stripes, he wanted you to know the important Democrats in office.

Regis put together a dinner party in September 1982 and invited a

Top: My friend
Bill Bennett.
Bottom: Secretary of
Energy Sam Bodman.
Top right: an Empower
America retreat
when I was chairman.
Bottom right: George
Schultz; Meg Whitman
and Condi Rice with
Jean and me

I was a delegate at the 2000 GOP convention and attended George W. Bush's Inauguration before I went to work for the new President.

Mr. Chips Goes to Washington

As if Floyd Kvamme didn't have enough influence, the Silicon Valley bigwig now has the ear of the most powerful man in the world. And, no, we're not talking about Alan Greenspan. Rather, President Bush has appointed Kvamme co-chair of the President's Council of Advisors on Science and Technology—or, as Bush will probably call it, "my group on math and stuff."

Kvamme, a partner at mega-venture capital firm Kleiner Perkins Caufield & Byers, will advise Bush on technology, scientific research, and math and scientific education. We are hoping there will also be a committee to advise Bush on grammar education.

The committee will consist of 12 people largely from the private sector. Along with his yet-to-be-appointed co-chair, Kvamme will have a hand in selecting the other members, so don't be surprised if the final list reads like a who's who of Valley luminaries.

While Kvamme has the résumé to support his appointment, his record as a generous Bush supporter even before the New Hampshire primary just goes to show that money does talk.

Kvamme denies that he's holding out for an ambassadorship or other higher post, saying only that he's "pleased to be able to serve." Kinda sounds like he'll be working in the White House kitchen.

Because the position is part-time and unpaid (like he needs the money), Kvamme has no plans to resign from Kleiner or relocate inside the Beltway. That's probably a wise thing: It's not good to show up your boss. —*Kent German*

Meeting with President Bush on Air Force One, in the White House,
and with the Bush family in Texas

To Floyd Kvamme
With best wishes,

To Jean and Floyd Kvamme
With best wishes,

number of Valley executives, including me. The purpose of the dinner was to drum up support for Jerry Brown's possible run for the White House in 1984. As the dinner drew to a close, Regis took pictures of each guest with his new auto-focus camera. As it turned out, all the pictures that Regis took that evening came out blurry because the auto-focus opted to focus on the back wall between the governor and the guest. After the event, we all chuckled about how accurate these photos really were—because, as one guest noted, "most things concerning Jerry Brown are a little fuzzy."

CHAPTER 51

Our Energy Future

ENERGY GENERATION THAT drives our economy has unfortunately become a political football. In this final chapter, I'll look at energy usage data gathered over a 25-year period stretching back to the period from 2001 to 2009 when I served as Co-Chair of the President's Council of Advisors on Science and Technology. During my eight years in the White House, no other subject attracted as much attention as did energy—the fuel to produce it, the production processes to make it user-friendly, and the environmental ramifications of its use.

As a starting point, the U.S. economy required about 100 quads of energy in each of the years between 2005 and 2020. That is 100 quadrillion BTUs. A BTU is approximately the amount of energy that gets released when you strike a match; a quadrillion is 1,000,000,000,000,000. About 40 percent of the energy generated was used to fuel our transportation, with mostly petroleum as its source; 40 percent was used to provide electricity sourced by nine different technologies (solar, nuclear, hydro, wind, geothermal, natural gas, coal, biomass, and small traces of petroleum); and 20 percent was used for sundry residential, commercial, and industrial applications.

When Congress passed the Energy Policy Act of 2005, we updated the manner in which we produced our electricity and fueled our transportation. In petroleum usage, our petroleum imports reached their maximum in 2005, at about 12.5 million barrels per day at prices peaking on occasion to above $100 per barrel. Something had to be done. The cost of energy was going to break the bank. Those sensitive to the environment called for a dramatic reduction in the use of fossil fuels (oil, coal, and natural gas), which accounted for over 80 percent of the energy source material. Others looked at the "clean" fuels and called for dramatic increases in the use of solar, wind, and other environmentally friendly sources such as geothermal and hydro.

Surprisingly, that 2005 legislation called for the restart of the nuclear industry and provided substantial incentives to power companies that would build new nuclear generating plants. In 2005, 104 nuclear plants were operating in the U.S., supplying slightly less than 20 percent of America's electricity. While the legislation called for the financial incentives to apply only to the next six plants to come online, some 30 proposals were submitted to build new nuclear generating capacity. This all changed with the failure of Japan's Fukushima power plant following an earthquake and tidal wave. Only one of these proposed plants, in Georgia, may now get to completion. A companion plant in South Carolina has been stopped.

So, what else has happened as a result of this landmark legislation? The use of coal has dropped from supplying about 23 percent of U.S. electric power to under 10% of our electricity. Coal has been replaced by natural gas as the fuel of choice for more than 30 percent of the nation's electricity. In 2005, natural gas supplied only 22% of our electricity. Since natural gas emits only about half of the CO_2 that coal does, this makes a significant change in the volume of CO_2 emissions.

The environmental movement has called for increases in solar and wind, but there's been little change in usage of these commodities in the 15-year period from 2005 to 2020. Solar increased from virtually nothing to currently supplying a little under 1% of America's electricity. Wind has gone from a tiny 0.15% position to supplying 2.5%—still small but up over 15 times its 2005 performance. One other interesting takeaway from the data is that the total amount of power utilized in the U.S. has stayed relatively flat at 100 quads due to the improved efficiency of generation.

When will there be more movement toward less fossil fuel usage? Before we see real traction of "green" alternatives, several issues need to be resolved:

1. Solar power is attractive since the fuel (the sun's rays) could be considered free. The problem is that solar-generated power is not cost-efficient. And there's the issue that the sun shines only for portions of a day. Using today's battery technology to store solar energy is expensive; in our study, we learned that it takes over three years for a photo-voltaic solar system to "pay back" the power it took to build the system. Those supporting an enormous increase in solar usage must answer this problem if they are to be taken seriously. I see solar continuing its use in small local systems for onsite generation but do not see the proposed growth in solar happening with any technology known today.

2. Electricity generation from wind has shown nice growth, but there are negatives. Wind blows only a portion of the day—frequently in the late afternoon when energy is least needed. Furthermore, wind is responsible for bird deaths, particularly raptors. On the positive side, wind generation equipment generally produces returns on investment in eight months. Again, however, proponents of massive increases in wind power will change the look of much of America. It is hard to imagine communities allowing such construction.

3. An area not discussed much but looking more attractive is biomass. When the 2005 legislation required gasoline fuels to contain a minimum of 10 percent ethanol, many people were surprised that ethanol production met America's demand. Ethanol is not a fossil fuel and enjoys a virtuous cycle by requiring the CO_2 that it generates to be consumed when the new crop is grown. Biomass is making attractive strides in energy areas such as aviation fuel.

4. The situation with nuclear energy is unfortunate. This clean base power-generating source was set for significant growth when the Fukushima disaster happened. Nuclear needs another serious look. It is the only power source that provides energy without any fossil fuel usage, and it has the best safety record of any fuel source.

5. We must get better at understanding the problems we might suffer if CO_2 emissions from fossil fuels continue to increase in the atmosphere. For instance, CO_2 enhances vegetation growth: This is why growers introduce CO_2 to levels of up to 1500ppm (parts per million) in hothouses (whereas CO_2 levels run about 420ppm in open land). And we must improve forecasting. In the early 1990s, we were told that by 2020 the earth's temperature would rise by up to three degrees Celsius if we reached certain CO_2 levels; the average temperature rose only about 20% of that. Moreover, we were told that sea levels would probably rise by 24 inches by 2020; at most reporting stations, sea levels have risen less than seven inches. It makes no scientific sense to continue to fret over climate policy until we clarify the real problems. The debates need to be driven by more and better data.

6. We have made real progress in energy usage. We are meeting the demands of a growing population, but there is more to do to improve energy efficiency. Hopefully, our policymakers and legislators will become more data driven and reward truth-telling—and dismiss energy fantasies that handicap progress by predicting the end of life as we know it.

Closing Comment

This is an amazing country. I have had the great pleasure of visiting more than 70 countries around the world. Many of these nations have magnificent features and wonderful people, but I have yet to find another "America." We are blessed with such a wide range of opportunities to invent, to innovate, to achieve. The variability of opportunities is made possible by the nature of 50 states and their individuality in climate, natural beauty, and overall environment, which allow for broad choice in living space and lifestyle. Whether you want urban or rural, crowded or spacious, no choice is off the table in this land of plenty. I've had the pleasure of living in bustling San Francisco, snowbound Syracuse, the suburbs of culture-rich Boston, crowded Los Angeles, the California coast, and booming Silicon Valley. I am a lucky man.

Appreciation

I thank my three sons—Mark, Damon, and Todd—and my friends and business associates of more than 60 years for helping me recall a very rich and rewarding life. Thanks also to SellersEaston Media for bringing structure to my story—particularly Pattie Sellers for her skillful interviewing and editing, and Samantha Kutz for her kind guidance through this literary production. While my wife of 61 years, Jean, is not with us to read A Silicon Valley Life, her spirit lives deep in the pages of this book. I thank Jean for our exciting journey together.

Printed in the United States of America First Printing, 2022

ISBN: 978-0-9994488-2-3

SellersEaston Media LLC
www.sellerseaston.com